HOODOO
BIBLE
MAGIC

Sacred Secrets of Scriptural Sorcery

Miss Michaele
and
Professor Charles Porterfield

Missionary Independent Spiritual Church
Forestville, California

→ 2014 ←

Hoodoo Bible Magic:
Sacred Secrets of Scriptural Sorcery
© 2014 by Michaele Maurer and Charles Porterfield
HoodooFoundry.com
ProfessorPorterfield.com

All rights reserved under International and Pan-American Copyright Conventions. No part of this publication can be reproduced, stored in a retrieval system, or transmitted in any format by any means, electronic, mechanical, photocopying, recording, or otherwise, without the written permission of the publisher.

Text:
Michaele Maurer, Charles Porterfield, catherine yronwode

Art:
Charles C. Dawson, Charles M. Quinlan, Unknown Artists

Cover:
Greywolf Townsend, Charles C. Dawson

Editor:
catherine yronwode

Production:
nagasiva yronwode, catherine yronwode, Charles Porterfield, Greywolf Townsend

Illustrations:
Bullet-Proof Bible from the Protecto Bible Co.   15
First Seal of Moses from the Sixth and Seventh Books of Moses   28
7th Pentacle of Jupiter from The Key of Solomon   31
Religious Goods Sold in Hoodoo Catalogues, 1934 - 2014   47

Some material in this book was first published at:
The Lucky Mojo Curio Company Forum: Forum.LuckyMojo.com
© 2009 - 2014 Lucky Mojo Curio Co. Used by permission.
The Association of Independent Readers and Rootworkers: ReadersAndRootworkers.org
© 2009 - 2014 Missionary Independent Spiritual Church. Used by permission.
Hoodoo Psychics, HoodooPsychics.com © 2011 - 2014 catherine yronwode, Miss Michaele, and Hoodoo Psychics. Used by permission.

First Edition 2014 - Second Edition 2016

Published by
Missionary Independent Spiritual Church
6632 Covey Road, Forestville, California 95436
MissionaryIndependent.org

ISBN10: 0-9960523-1-3 / ISBN13: 978-0-9960523-1-3

Printed in Canada.

Contents

Dedication and Acknowledgments 4
In the Beginning 5
    The Bible Comes to Hoodoo 5
    Is Magic Incompatible with the Bible? 6
    Heroes of the Bible Work Magical Spells 7
        Jacob, Joseph, Joshua, Moses, Aaron, Miriam, Elijah, and Solomon 7
        Jesus the Master of Magic 14
    Doctors, Conjurers, Faithful Disciples 15
        Sketches of Christian Rootworkers 15
        The Conjure Doctor as Church Leader 16
        Spiritual Church Mediums 18
Forget Not All His Benefits 21
    The Bible Itself is a Magical Book 21
        Burning, Boiling, and Bathing 22
        The Bible Stops a Bullet 24
        Bible Amulets and Charms: Mizpahs, Midget Bibles, and Mezuzot 26
    Scriptural Magic 29
        Selected Scriptures for Magical Use 30
        7 Bible Verses that Show God is Listening 31
        Pleading the Blood of Jesus 32
    Psalmic Magic 33
        The Book of Psalms in Folk Magic 36
        A Quick List of the 150 Psalms and Their Uses 38
        You Can Do Anything with Psalms 23 42
        The "Chicago Psalms" 44
        7 Deadly Bible Psalms to Quell Your Foes 46
        8 Powerful Psalms to Reverse and Send Back Evil 47
    Divinatory Magic 48
        Bibliomantic Cleidomancy 48
        Biblical Bibliomancy 49
        Dream Books and the Bible 50
    Devotionary Magic 51
        A Practical Guide to Prayer: How Shall We Pray? 51
        Preaching as Prayer 52
        A Curse in a Baptist Sermon: Hitler and Hell 54
Bible Spells Old and New 58
    Steady Work, Money, Success, Gambling 58
    Recovering People and Goods 62
    Love, Family, Reconciliation 63
    Helping, Blessing, and Healing 67
    Harming and Cursing 72
    Protection and Jinx-Breaking 74
At the End 80
    Frequently Asked Questions 80
    One Last Curiosity: The Soldier's Bible 94
Bibliography 96

Dedication

This book is dedicated to all the prophets, sages, apostles, saints, and mages who have gone before — and will come after.

"I bind unto myself the power of the great love of Cherubim; the sweet 'Well done' in judgment hour; the service of the Seraphim; Confessors' faith, Apostles' word, the Patriarchs' prayers, the Prophets' scrolls; all good deeds done unto the Lord, and purity of virgin souls."
— St. Patrick's Breastplate, translated by Cecil Frances Alexander

Acknowledgements

The authors would like to gratefully acknowledge the following people for their contributions to this book:

Harry Maurer: Loyal husband, driver, right-hand man, and asker of thoughtful questions. Without his kind assistance this book would not have been possible.

Charles and Helen Jones, of blessed memory: Beloved grandparents.

Christy Porterfield: Dearest thanks to a divine wife and patient councilor.

Thanks also to our editor catherine yronwode, the pastor of Missionary Independent Spiritual Church and co-proprietress of the Lucky Mojo Curio Company, who granted us access to her collection of rare books and pamphlets and supplied suggestions for many of the topics covered herein, and to her husband nagasiva yronwode for his help with technical matters and book production.

Thanks to Greywolf Townsend for his cover art and interior illustrations, developed in loving homage to the inimitable artist Charles C. Dawson.

Thanks to the many rootworkers, both those named in the text and those whose names have regrettably been lost, who generously instructed Newbell Niles Puckett and Rev. Harry M. Hyatt in the art of conjure from 1925 through 1940 — and to those estimable folklorists for recording the information.

We also extend the hand of gratitude to the creative members of the Lucky Mojo Forum for asking such insightful questions and to the moderation team — especially Aura Laforest, Mama Micki, Joseph Magnuson, Miss Tammie Lee, Miss Aida, and Papa Newt — for posting such consistently helpful replies.

Finally, many answers to questions, as well as favourite Bible spells provided herein, came to us from our wonderful colleagues in AIRR, the Association of Independent Readers and Rootworkers: ConjureMan Ali, Lukianos, Mary Bee, Miss Bri, Ms. Melanie, and Professor Ames.

In the Beginning

THE BIBLE COMES TO HOODOO

"A word fitly spoken is like apples of gold in pictures of silver."
— Proverbs 25:11

The Bible and Christianity entered the African Diaspora during difficult times, but became so enmeshed with the folk beliefs of conjure practice that the two are now inseparable. Just as our knowledge of Scriptures does not come from one source, so too our knowledge of rootwork is not limited to a single voice, book, or place. It comes instead from people who daily lived their beliefs and practices of prayer and magic.

Much of this history has been preserved by folklorists, community record keepers, archivists, and manufacturers of spiritual supplies. These individuals helped bring that knowledge across time to us. Thanks to them, in some cases we know not only where long-passed practitioners lived, but also their names and professions. They live on in their words.

Books such as ours would scarcely be possible without the work of our forerunners. A handful of them stand out to us, particularly for what they have preserved of the religious aspects of hoodoo:

- Newbell Niles Puckett, educator, sociologist, and folklorist whose *Folk Beliefs of the Southern Negro* was published in 1926.
- Folklorist and novelist Zora Neale Hurston who in the 1930s wrote *Hoodoo in America*, *Mules and Men*, and *Moses Man of the Mountain*.
- Lewis de Claremont, the pseudonymous owner of Oracle Products and author of the 1936 book *Legends of Incense, Herb, and Oil Magic*.
- Henri Gamache, the pseudonymous author of *The Master Book of Candle Burning* and *8th, 9th, and 10th Books of Moses* in the 1940s.
- Sydney J. R. Steiner, a.k.a. Mikhail Strabo, proprietor of Guidance House and author of the 1942 *Magic Formula for Successful Prayer*.
- The Rev. Harry M. Hyatt, amateur folklorist, whose *Hoodoo - Conjuration - Witchcraft - Rootwork* was published in the 1970s.

This continues on today with such sources as Yvonne Chireau's 2003 *Black Magic: Religion and the African American Conjuring Tradition* and Jeffrey E. Anderson's 2007 *Conjure in African American Society*.

We are indebted to them all.

IS MAGIC INCOMPATIBLE WITH THE BIBLE?

"In the beginning God created the heaven and the earth."

— Genesis 1:1

As we see from the Biblical quotation above, the Holy Scriptures themselves begin with the greatest of all magical acts; the creation of existence by God. The Scriptures contain countless examples of magic, miracles, wonders, dreams, visions, and prophecies, and they have been used throughout the ages as a guide, instruction manual, formulary, comfort giver, enemy thwarter, and constant companion.

However, at various times and places the use of the Holy Scriptures in magic has come under fire by ecclesiastic authorities. The conventional view of magic in some modern churches is one of unremitting and invariable condemnation. For this reason, many assume that magic of all kinds is forbidden by God. Some people have even told us that they were drawn to magic, in part, because their experience with Christianity had been painful or emotionally damaging and that to practice magic was a personal declaration of independence or a vital part of their healing and personal growth.

To all of our readers who love magic but were taught that there is no such a thing as biblical Jewish and Christian spell-casting, we bring you the good news: the Bible does in fact contain accounts of magic, the Bible has been used by devout Jews and Christians to perform magic, and the books of the Bible — the actual written scrolls and printed pages — are themselves magical!

Some may disagree with this and with what we teach herein. In the end this book is simply what we have been taught and guided to, not an ultimate authority. The ultimate authority is God alone. Some may even try and turn you away from the secrets that we offer you here; they may seek to deny you the blessings and powers that are rightfully yours from God, but remember: *"The devil can cite Scripture for his purpose."*

So in the words of Isaiah 52:1 we say to each of you reading this: *"Awake, awake; put on thy strength, O Zion; put on thy beautiful garments, O Jerusalem."* Come and light your glowing candles, burn your fragrant incense, and open your household altars to the beauty and power of the Magic in the Bible!

HEROES OF THE BIBLE WORK MAGICAL SPELLS

In the Bible there are many instances of magic and spell work, but they have been blurred by religious dogmatism and obscured by the mists of history and no longer seem to be the kinds of acts that most people mean when they say "magic spells." Please allow us to remind you of them here:

[handwritten: Now I understand why I loved the stories of the Bible.]

MAGICAL TRADITIONS REGARDING JACOB

In the Book of Genesis, we read that Jacob, the son of Isaac, worked for Laban, the brother of Rebecca and brother-in-law of Isaac, for 14 years to pay the bride-price for his two daughters Leah and Rachel. Jacob then struck a bargain with Laban to provide for his household after he had fulfilled his contract. In Genesis 30:31, Jacob asked for no money, but said:

"I will pass through all thy flock to day, removing from thence all the speckled and spotted cattle, and all the brown cattle among the sheep, and the spotted and speckled among the goats: and of such shall be my hire."

Laban agreed, but Jacob took fresh-cut branches of poplar, hazel, and chestnut and peeled their bark back, making white stripes and streaks on the branches. He placed these branches in the watering troughs, so Laban's flocks would see them while they drank. When they mated, the sheep and goats then bore streaked, speckled, and spotted young, which Jacob added to his claim and thus magically increased his flocks.

[handwritten: conjuring #1]

MAGICAL TRADITIONS REGARDING JOSEPH

Genesis 40-41 tells us that during Joseph's sojourn in Egypt he revealed a gift for dream interpretation. While in prison for a crime he did not commit, he correctly interpreted the prophetic dreams of two fellow inmates: one of exaltation, the other of execution. Eventually this gift earned him his freedom when Pharaoh had a dream that defied all his soothsayers: seven healthy cattle came up out of the river, only to be eaten up by seven emaciated cattle. Joseph not only correctly foretold that the dream was a prophecy of seven years of bumper crops followed by seven years of famine, but he also created a plan to avert the disaster by building up Egypt's grain reserves during the prosperous years to stave off the famine years. For this he was exalted to high office by Pharaoh.

MAGICAL TRADITIONS REGARDING AARON

In Exodus 7:8-12, and Numbers 17:8, we learn of Aaron's mighty rod. Moses and Aaron went before Pharaoh to perform a miracle. Aaron cast down his rod at Pharaoh's feet and it became a serpent. Pharaoh had his magicians duplicate the feat, but Aaron's serpent devoured the others:

"And Moses and Aaron went in unto Pharaoh, and they did so as the Lord had commanded: and Aaron cast down his rod before Pharaoh, and before his servants, and it became a serpent.

Then Pharaoh also called the wise men and the sorcerers: now the magicians of Egypt, they also did in like manner with their enchantments.

For they cast down every man his rod, and they became serpents: but Aaron's rod swallowed up their rods."

Later the Lord ordered that each of the Twelve Tribes provide a rod, and that the rod of the tribe chosen to become the priests of the Tabernacle would miraculously sprout overnight. Aaron provided his rod on behalf of the tribe of Levi, and once planted in the ground, *"it put forth buds, produced blossoms, and bore ripe almonds."*

Aaron's rod bore on one side sweet almonds, and on the other side bitter almonds. If the Israelites obeyed the Lord, the sweet almonds would ripen and be edible, but if they forsook the Lord the bitter almonds would propagate.

MAGICAL TRADITIONS REGARDING JOSHUA

In the Book of Joshua, Chapter 6, we learn that the Lord declared in advance that Joshua would conquer the city of Jericho, and gave him instructions for a seven-day spell: Once a day for six days the army of the Jews marched around the city with the priests in the lead, carrying the Ark of the Covenant, and blowing rams' horns. On the seventh day they marched around the city seven times in the same formation, thus making a total of 13 marches around the city.

"And it came to pass at the seventh time, when the priests blew with the trumpets, Joshua said unto the people, Shout; for the LORD hath given you the city. ... So the people shouted when the priests blew with the trumpets: and ... the wall fell down flat, so that the people went up into the city, every man straight before him, and they took the city."

MAGICAL TRADITIONS CONCERNING MOSES

Moses is best known as the author of the first five books of the Bible, the Great Lawgiver and Liberator of the Israelites. The most famous figure in Biblical magic outside of Jesus, he is also the attributed author of the 6th through the 10th lost books of Moses and *The Sword of Moses*. There is not enough space here to list all of his great acts; we will however say this of him: From the bulrushes to the court of great Pharaoh, from the burning desert to the burning bush, from the plagues to the Passover, from the striking of the tablets to the striking of the rock, Moses did it all!

GRIMOIRES ATTRIBUTED TO HEROES OF THE BIBLE

"How could African-American slaves or their descendants have access to esoteric European tracts and grimoires? The answer is stunningly simple: They bought them by mail order and read them."

— catherine yronwode

A grimoire is a book of spells, divinations, and instructions for making magical talismans and amulets, and may provide rituals for summoning angels, spirits, or demons. Not all grimoires are biblical, but there are quite a few whose authorship is attributed to great figures of the Bible. When the Rev. Harry M. Hyatt interviewed 1,600 African-American rootworkers in the South from 1936 to 1940, he found that many of them owned such grimoires. Typically sold through mail order catalogues, these manuals on spell-craft were widely advertised in black-owned newspapers such as the *Chicago Defender*. To this day, African-American spiritual workers continue to consult biblical grimoires like *The Secrets of the Psalms, The 6th and 7th Books of Moses, Mystery of the Long Lost 8th, 9th, and 10th Books of Moses*, and old German-American mystical standards such as *Pow-Wows or the Long Lost Friend*, and *Albertus Magnus Egyptian Secrets*.

If you peruse a grimoire attributed to an ancient figure of the Bible such as Moses or Solomon, it becomes apparent that the book was not the work of the great name assigned to it, but something wholly other. Such false attribution typically occurred for one of two reasons. Either the original author's name was forgotten or a little known writer credited his work to a legendary figure in hopes of attracting attention, publicity, or sales.

THE 6TH AND 7TH BOOKS OF MOSES

The Sixth and Seventh Books of Moses or Moses' Magical Spirit-Art is a magical text attributed to Moses, the author of the first five books of the Bible. Supposedly a hidden adjunct to the Bible, it purports to instruct the reader in the spells used to create the miracles of the Bible. It includes magical drawings or seals accompanied by incantations that instruct one on how to perform a variety of spell-casting feats, from controlling weather and people to contacting the dead, including famous Biblical figures.

No first edition of the book has been discovered, but 18th-century German pamphlet versions do exist. After an 1849 printing of the book caught the public fancy, the use of the Mosaic seals in folk magic spread through Germany and Northern Europe and then to German immigrants in the United States. As soon as the text was translated into English, it was picked up by African-American root doctors in the South as well as Afro-West-Indian obeah practitioners. The book was actually banned in Jamaica, adding to its mystique. A favourite reference that demonstrates this is the 1963 song *"Six And Seven Books Of Moses"* by the Jamaican reggae group the Maytals. The band's leader, "Toots" Hibbert, a former gospel singer, first lists the canonical books of the Old Testament, but he ends with *"... the Sixth and the Seventh books, they wrote them all."*

The First Seal of Moses, from the *Sixth and Seventh Books of Moses*.

THE LONG LOST 8TH, 9TH, AND 10TH BOOKS OF MOSES

Originally published in 1945, *Mystery of the Long Lost 8th, 9th, and 10th Books of Moses* was written by Henri Gamache, the author of such hoodoo classics as *The Master Book of Candle Burning* and *Terrors of the Evil Eye Exposed*. Gamache is one of the most mysterious figures in conjure, variously identified as a pseudonym for the occult shop owner and publisher Joseph Spitalnick, a.k.a. Joe Kay, or "a young Jewish woman who did the research and wrote the books" for Kay.

Gamache appears to have collected the material for this work from Medieval and Middle Eastern grimoires, mixed them liberally with the radically Afro-centric socio-political theories of Marcus Garvey, summarized portions of Zora Neale Hurston's book *Moses Man of the Mountain,* and then attributed the whole package to Moses the Lawgiver.

This book departs drastically from the grimoire style of the earlier *6th and 7th Books of Moses*. The text begins with an astounding biography in which Moses' life is used to show that African tribal beliefs are linked to ancient Jewish and Egyptian religions. The second part of the book is a discourse on how the sacred writings of Moses were lost. The volume ends with the 44 Secret Keys to Universal Power, some of them translated from a German edition of the *Greek Magical Papyri* and some from a then very obscure grimoire called *The Sword of Moses,* which had earlier been translated into German by a scholar named Moses Gaster. Whoever Henri Gamache was, he or she certainly could read German fluently.

In Gamache's view, Moses was "The Great Voodoo Man of the Bible," and Gamache departed from Biblical tradition in others ways as well. For instance, the Bible only briefly mentions Jethro, high priest of Midian and Moses' father-in-law, but Gamache suggests that Jethro possessed great secrets which Moses studied until he could turn water into blood, command the power of flame, bring disease to cattle, and create swarms of insects; in short, until he had the Ten Plagues in the palm of his hand.

Gamache freely admitted that the spells and seals passed down under the name of Moses were not Moses' work, but said that even after the original meaning of the text was lost, miracles and wonders still occurred. Gamache put forth that the seals' "non-Hebraic origin does not detract from their authority." In other words, Moses may not have composed them, said Gamache, but they have enough power to be worthy of his name.

MAGICAL TRADITIONS REGARDING MIRIAM

The sister of Moses is the subject of the Bible's short, potent, "Five Word Prayer": *"O Lord, make her well."* She is associated with the protective Hand of Miriam amulet against the evil eye and with the old Sephardic Jewish healing spell, *"Like Miriam, the prophetess, who performed cures and gave medicine and took away all the sickness and threw it into the depths of the sea, so I take away the sickness of so-and-so, daughter of such-and-such."*

MAGICAL TRADITIONS REGARDING ELIJAH

* Read more About

Elijah the Prophet raised the dead, caused and remedied a great drought, and was taken up in a fiery chariot. A harbinger of the Messiah, he is prophesied to return, *"Before the coming of the great and terrible day of the Lord."* In one old Sephardic spell Elijah banishes the evil eye from a nursing mother and tells her to *"breast-feed your children with joy."*

MAGICAL TRADITIONS REGARDING SOLOMON

Solomon Henri Anderson Patton

King Solomon (970 to 931 BCE), the son of King David, is the subject of the Biblical books of *Kings* and *Chronicles* and was the author of the *Song of Songs* (said to describe his love affair with the Queen of Sheba), the *Book of Proverbs, Ecclesiastes,* and the apocryphal *Wisdom of Solomon.*

Solomon not only oversaw the building of the First Temple and established Jerusalem as a city of justice and peace, he was a powerful ruler and a wise judge. He was also said to have been a sorcerer who could communicate with and command the allegiance of animals, demons, and the dead. As such he was posthumously credited with the authorship of several grimoires, including the 14th-15th century *Key of Solomon the King* and the 17th century *Lesser Key of Solomon.*

Through the same sales agencies that brought the Seals of Moses into hoodoo, Solomonic-style spells to control demonic and spiritual forces by means of talismanic seals and sigils were accepted and adapted by 20th century rootworkers. The use of these seals, in conjunction with prayers, became very common among those engaged in the making of mojo bags, and they were also carried in the pocket or wallet. Solomon's name even graces the classic hoodoo oil, King Solomon Wisdom.

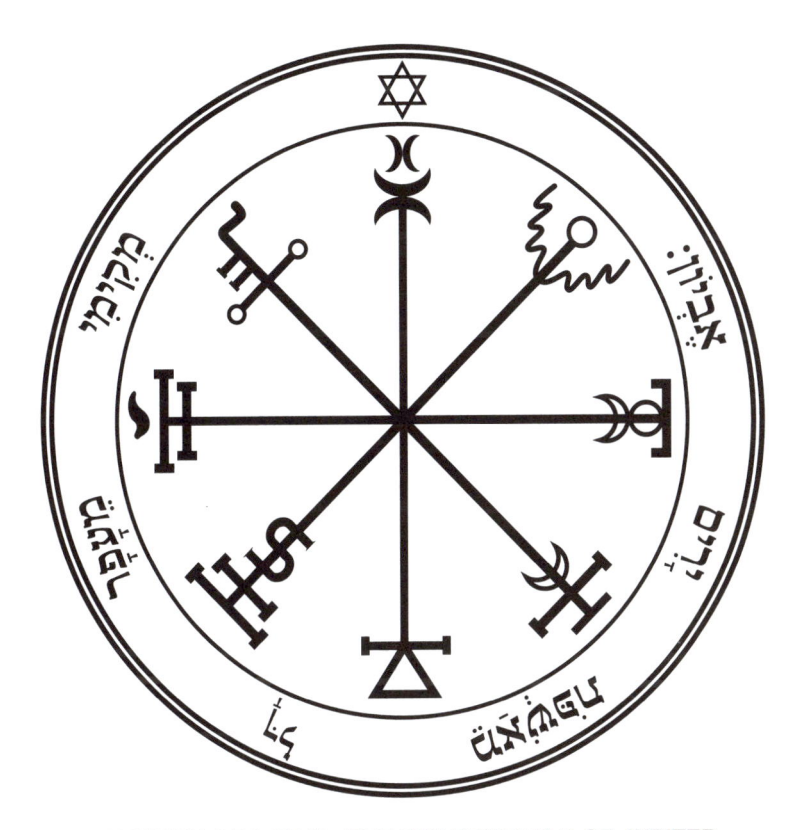

ANATOMY OF A SEAL: THE 7TH PENTACLE OF JUPITER

According to *The Key of Solomon the King,* as translated into English by S. L. McGregor Mathers, this seal "hath great power against poverty, if thou considerest it with devotion, repeating the versicle. It serveth furthermore to drive away those spirits who guard treasures, and to discover the same." At the top is the Shield or Star of David for strength and protection. The eight radiating lines form a magical symbol that goes back to ancient Babylon; similar emblems are also found in Norse magic. At the terminals are mystical symbols drawn from Renaissance Christian ceremonial magic that are intended to express, attract, and command the benevolent planetary forces of Jupiter. The Hebrew versicle around the circle looks more mysterious than it actually is: The text is from Psalms 113:7-8: *"He raiseth up the poor out of the dust, and lifteth the needy out of the dunghill; That he may set him with princes, even with the princes of his people."*

JESUS THE MASTER OF MAGIC

> "But when the Pharisees heard it, they said, This fellow doth not cast out devils, but by Beelzebub the prince of the devils.
> And Jesus knew their thoughts, and said unto them, Every kingdom divided against itself is brought to desolation; and every city or house divided against itself shall not stand:
> And if Satan cast out Satan, he is divided against himself; how shall then his kingdom stand? And if I by Beelzebub cast out devils, by whom do your children cast them out? Therefore they shall be your judges.
> But if I cast out devils by the Spirit of God, then the kingdom of God is come unto you."
>
> – Matthew 12:24-28

For the most part, Jesus' mere words were sufficient to work miracles. He could turn water into wine, heal paralysis, curse a tree, multiply loaves and fishes, or bring a dead person back to life. His power included the most potent of spiritual abilities to cast out, dismiss, or quell evil spirits. This power remains inherent in the gift of Jesus" delivering blood.

To heal the sick on three different occasions he resorted to an old folk cure that employs the protective and healing properties of saliva. You spit three times to ward off the effects of a curse, and it is a sovereign cure for eye diseases. This tradition was already ancient in Jesus' lifetime, and in the Second Temple period there was also a belief that the saliva of a legitimate firstborn son had healing properties. (You will also find this belief stated, without any additional detail, in the *The Sixth and Seventh Books of Moses.*) Because some who saw Jesus thought that he was an illegitimate son, it stands to reason that his healing the sick with spit would have been an effective counterargument against those who questioned the legitimacy of his birth.

- **Mark 7:33:** To heal a deaf and mute man, Jesus stuck his fingers in the man's ears, spat, and touched the man's tongue.
- **Mark 8:23:** Jesus spat on a blind man's eyes, touched the man's eyes, and restored his sight.
- **John 9:6:** Jesus spat on the ground to make a small quantity of mud to smear over another blind man's eyes to return his sight.

DOCTORS, CONJURERS, FAITHFUL DISCIPLES

"Is any sick among you? Let him call for the elders of the church; and let them pray over him, anointing him with oil in the name of the Lord."

— James 5:14

SKETCHES OF CHRISTIAN ROOTWORKERS

The bond between the root doctor and the church is deep and abiding. In his 5-volume *Hoodoo Conjuration Witchcraft Rootwork,* published from 1970-1978, the Rev. Harry M. Hyatt related stories of his 1930s tour of the South, where he interviewed rootworking ministers and preachers. He was given dozens of spells that called for the recitation of Scripture; were performed in the names of the Trinity or the Apostles; or made physical use of the Bible, Holy Oil, or Holy Water. As one professional conjure doctor told him, "You know the Lord Jesus Christ is the biggest hoodoo man in the world. You got to have him to go along with you to do these things."

Jim Haskins, in his 1978 book *Voodoo and Hoodoo: the Craft as Revealed by Traditional Practitioners,* noted that "the Baptist Church was particularly attractive to the slaves, for certain aspects of its practice were identifiable with African religious traditions." And Jeffrey E. Anderson cited the same linkages in his 2001 book *Conjure in African American Society:* "Some hoodoo doctors were specially gifted with the ability to conjure by God or spirits, as had been their African forebears." The same is true today.

MRS. MYRTLE COLLINS, THE ROSICRUCIAN ROOT DOCTOR

Mrs. Myrtle Collins, a professional root doctor of Memphis, Tennessee, who worked with herbs and had received training from a Rosicrucian order, took the Christian basis of her work very seriously. As she told Rev. Hyatt during her interview with him in 1938: *"I'm a spiritual doctor. I know about this work. I'm a 'doctor' that 'tricks.' The sacrifice that you offer up to Jesus removes the 'trick', for he is the 'trick giver' and the 'trick taker.'*

"You consecrate your altar with a prayer. In that room I wear white robes. I wear a white satin hat. It's a cap-like. It just fits your head. That protects [you against] the work [turning] your hair [...] gray. This work will age you."

She also told him, "We get plenty of work from white people."

THE CONJURE DOCTOR AS CHURCH LEADER

The majority of African-American rootworkers are Protestants, with the Baptist denominations in the fore. We will now see that conjure doctors who deal exclusively with good spirits are often also Baptist church leaders.

ALLEN VAUGHN

A fine conjure doctor who was also a church leader was Allen Vaughn of North Carolina. Not only was he a conjure man of great repute, but he also conducted prayer meetings and sat on the mourner's bench of the Menola Baptist Church.

Born into slavery, Vaughn became an influential figure in his community soon after the Civil War ended in 1865. During this period, small prayer groups of ex-slaves were developing community churches. As the historian F. Roy Johnson described it, *"The free people, impatient to begin their own meetings, at times gathered beneath groves to listen to leaders and preachers, then erected bush shelters against adverse weather."* The Menola Baptist Church first began beneath such a bush arbor.

During these years Vaughn gained recognition as a good herb doctor who also read fortunes by cutting cards. Vaughn's patients received physical and spiritual treatments for their ailments. According to one of his patients, he would *"give them medicine to ease pain, and pull the tricks to ease their mind."*

He was not only a respected root doctor and a trick doctor, but also extended his leadership to church affairs. Alfred Futrell of Menola, North Carolina said of Vaughn:

"Allen was a good conjure doctor, and in those days, until about 40 years following the Civil War, they went to him, church folks and all ... a Christian man and a floor member of the Menola Baptist Church."

Allen Vaughn was one of the first to instruct his nephew, the fabled Doctor Jim Jordan, in the art of conjure and as a result of Vaughn's influence and instruction, Doctor Jordan's early practice was patterned largely after Vaughn's practice. Not only did Vaughn educate his nephew in conjure work, he also taught his own son James "Jim" Frank Vaughn and his daughter Josephine "Aunt Jo" Minton, both of whom went on to become respected conjure professionals in their own time.

THE FABLED DOCTOR JIM JORDAN

Born in Murfreesboro, North Carolina to a Baptist family that included many famous conjure workers, Doctor Jim Jordan (1871 - 1962) is perhaps one of the most well-known of the conjure church leaders.

His father Isaac Jordan, born in slavery in 1845, was a lay preacher at the Mill Neck Baptist Church in Como, North Carolina. Isaac Jordan conducted prayer meetings and led church services, and in later years pastored Mt. Gilean Church in Virginia. Dr. Jordan was himself a member of Mill Neck Baptist Church, as well as the Knights of Pythias, the Order of Love and Charity, and the Ahoskie Masonic Lodge.

Jim Jordan's mother, Harriet Hill Jordan, born in slavery in 1839, was of mixed African and Native American descent, and taught her children the medical properties of local herbs. Jordan also learned conjuring and divination techniques from his father's brother, Allen Vaughn.

At Mill Neck Church, Jim Jordan was well respected. *"He would shake hands, talk to all alike ... floor members, deacons, and preacher. He'd always ask folks how they were getting along."* However, his friends told "strange stories" of him: The doctor, it was said, could *"cast off spells, get you out of trouble, find things, perform magic, and treat with medicine."* Dr. Jordan collaborated with root doctors, faith healers, and occult shops in New York, Philadelphia, and Baltimore; clients travelled cross-country to see him.

His biographer and decades-long friend, F. Roy Johnson, included in his book *The Fabled Doctor Jim Jordan, a Story of Conjure* the following short biography and fond tribute to Dr. Jordan after his death:

"James Spurgeon (Jim) Jordan, one of the more successful conjure doctors of the past century, said he never joined forces with 'Ole Satan;' instead he 'walked beside de Lord' rendering help to people in the measure needed. [...] This man gained national recognition among conjure clientele [and lived] 90 years. [...] A large majority of his more prominent acquaintances characterized him as an honest and liberal man [...] Admiration was shared by medical doctors, business and professional people, and law enforcement authorities."

In the end we hear from F. Roy Johnson that when Dr. Jim Jordan passed away, *"A large crowd honoured him by attending his funeral at Mill Neck Baptist Church Wednesday afternoon, January 31, [1962], with Pastor Mitchell officiating."*

SPIRITUAL CHURCH MEDIUMS

Historically African-American Spiritualist churches trace their lineage back to 19th century American Spiritualism. In 1922, the National Spiritualist Association of Churches enforced a policy of racial segregation, and expelled en masse from the NSAC. The Black Spiritualists then formed the Colored Spiritualist Association of Churches. Over the years the CSAC schismed and became defunct, leaving in its place a loose confederation of denominations as well as many independent and non-denominational churches, collectively known as the Spiritual Church Movement.

Within these denominations, there are several forms of Judeo-Christian liturgical style, including elements of Catholicism, Protestantism, and a mixture of both. Many include recognizable elements of African Diasporic ancestral traditions, and some hold services in honour of specific non-Christian spirits and spirit guides, such as the Sauk leader Black Hawk, a Native American warrior of the late 18th and early 19th centuries. These churches may hold mediumship training courses, and their programs may include instruction in psychic reading, scrying, and crystal ball gazing. Their pastors may lead members in prayers, contact with ancestor spirits, candle work at the altar, and even casting spells of beneficial magic that are identical to those found within hoodoo folk-magic.

MOTHERS LEAFY ANDERSON AND CATHERINE SEALS

One of the most famous leaders of the Spiritual Church Movement was Mother Leafy Anderson. She founded several churches in the 1920s, the most prominent being in New Orleans, Louisiana. She worked with traditional spirit guides and Christian iconography in worship services, but Black Hawk was her personal spirit guide, and the church offered special services and hymns that honored him. Upon her death, Black Hawk became the spirit guide of her successor, Mother Catherine Seals.

Mother Seals led The Temple of Innocent Blood until her death, after which it fractured, giving rise to a multiplicity of Spiritualist denominations in New Orleans. After the death of Mother Seals, Black Hawk made his presence known to many within the Spiritual Church Movement, and passed from the category of a personal spirit guide to that of a powerful working spirit who answers all who petition him for aid.

DOCTOR BUZZARD'S BROTHER, THE SPIRITUALIST

In 1938 Rev. Hyatt was in New Orleans, where he interviewed a cousin of the noted hoodoo mesmerist Dr. Julius P. Caesar. Caesar's cousin, also a rootworker, told Hyatt of a preacher he knew who was supposedly the brother of the great Dr. Buzzard, the famed conjure worker of Beaufort, South Carolina. That led Hyatt to ask his informant if preachers, at least some of them, did hoodoo work. The informant explained:

"That's the idea — you grasp the idea — some do and some don't. Now, there is some of 'em deal direct with nothing but the Bible. Then, they got some of 'em do clairvoyant work, or all that kind of stuff. They make hands, you know, fix you up a little bag, and put some Cayenne Pepper and different stuff in there and tell you to go ahead and wear it, why you going to have luck. Then they got some of 'em actually can fix a hand up with a Lucky Bean, so it has a tendency to make a man go ahead and have luck."

Next, he described the kind of Spiritualist healing service that the man he knew as Dr. Buzzard's brother held with his congregation:

"They always have what you call Twelve Disciples, just as Jesus Christ had. They line up around their Mother [the female leader or Mother of the Church], why, they'd sing hymns, you know."

The healing invitation would go out: "Whosomever have pain about their body, come in the healing circle. ... They'd all get in there and just get round 'em like that." Those in the circle were rubbed down by the disciples, who would flick the pain away like drops of water. The healed persons would then be invited to testify about the relief they received.

He went on to explain that after taking up and praying over a collection, "they coming out to broadcast" — that is, to tell fortunes or demonstrate mediumship. "Well, they'll line up around there — all get in a line like that, and they'll just sing a hymn." Once "the spirit's going in 'em," the leader might come up to someone and say, for instance, "Have you got a sister named Dinah, or Louise, or Sadie in the other world?"

Some of the readers at church were "weak" and had to fish for names, offering up generic messages. Others were not weak at all: "But some of 'em are good, will come right up to you and tell you, 'I get you. Have you got a brother named Andrew Mitchell? I see him far off. He's not dead — he seems to be far off in Texas. ... And your brother is roaming around in trouble and you'll get a letter in three days.' You get that letter in three days, too."

A SUPPLY HOUSE REMEMBERS DR. KING

A final example of the connection between the conjure doctor and the preacher comes to us from more recent times, and demonstrates the unbroken tradition of Judeo-Christian conjure.

In 1933 Morris Shapiro left Keystone Laboratories, which he had co-founded in 1923 with Hubert Menke, to found Lucky Heart Laboratories. Both companies were headquartered in Memphis, Tennessee, and both manufactured hoodoo spiritual supplies as well as cosmetics suited to the African-American market. These products were marketed nationwide and both companies advertised heavily in the national black press. Additionally, both companies recruited networks of sales agents from within the African-American community.

Although Shapiro and Menke were Jewish, Keystone Laboratories helped to sponsor and promote the Pentecostal Church of God in Christ at their annual conventions in Memphis, while Lucky Heart Laboratories became inextricably associated with the Baptist Church.

In 1968 the great civil rights activist and Baptist minister, the Rev. Dr. Martin Luther King, Jr., whom many saw as the Moses of his day, was staying at the Lorraine Motel in Memphis, Tennessee, directly across the street from the Lucky Heart offices. It was at the Lorraine Motel, on April 4, 1968 at 6:01 p.m. that a shot rang out into the evening air and the Rev. Dr. Martin Luther King, Jr. fell to an assassin's bullet.

In the days after the assassination, the grief of the nation almost sundered it with riots, looting, and violence. In time the moral outrage and anger gave way to the peace so beloved by the Rev. Dr. King.

In the years following Rev. Dr. King's assassination, Walter Bailey, the motel's owner, maintained rooms 306 and 307, the rooms in front of which the assassination had taken place, as a memorial to Dr. King.

By the early 1980s the Lorraine Motel was facing foreclosure. In December of 1982 the motel was sold to the newly formed Martin Luther King Memorial Foundation. The funds raised to establish this foundation included a $10,000 donation from the Lucky Heart Company. The Lorraine Motel is now the National Civil Rights Museum.

To this day you will still find the framed picture of Dr. King, usually alongside those of John and Robert Kennedy, proudly displayed in many conjure, hoodoo, curio, and candle shops, as well as on private altars.

Forget Not All His Benefits

THE BIBLE ITSELF IS A MAGICAL BOOK

"Heaven and earth shall pass away: but my words shall not..."
— Mark 13:31

Written magic has existed almost as long as there has been writing. We see it in Egyptian papyri, Roman cursing tablets, Hebrew prayers inside mezuzot, Mayan codices, ancient tablets reproduced in *The Long-Lost 8th, 9th, and 10th Books of Moses,* and, yes, in the Bible itself!

In these days of near universal literacy, we have long forgotten how strange it is that living speech — declarations of love, threats of war, lies, rumours, confessions, curses, blessings, and stories of miracles — can be reduced to mute marks on paper and then brought back to life by those who know the art of reading. Remember that during the Middle Ages the act of reading silently to oneself was viewed with suspicion and fear, for it was seen as a magical act in and of itself.

All of this is only a small part of the reason that the Bible and other books of Scripture are objects of power. Joshua Trachtenberg, author of *Jewish Magic and Superstition,* explains it this way:

"[The Bible's] virtue has consisted primarily in divine origin. It speaks in the voice of God [...] It possesses something of the personality and attributes of deity. And so there grow up schools of mystical and esoteric exegesis which profess to discover the hidden inner significance of the Word [...] not only is it the word of the Lord, it is the Lord himself..."

We are taught that one does not steal or deface a Bible. When writing out a portion of Scripture for use in conjure, do not tear out a page from your Bible! It is tempting to print out verses from the internet, but we believe you should instead hand-copy your portion onto paper and finish with the name of the specific book, chapter, and verse from which it is quoted. After this, your name or command can be written as a "signature" at the end of the verse, around it in a circle or square, or atop it, either criss-cross or running over the lines of Scripture.

As we will see later, such a hand-copied portion of Scripture may be used to contain personal concerns or even be burnt to obtain "Bible ashes." But never do we destroy or obliterate a Bible.

BURNING, BOILING, AND BATHING

Portions of Scripture contain inherent power, and thus they can be used in many ways. They can be recited aloud over people, herbs, oils, or curios; inscribed on candles; written out on petitions, prayers, or papers; dissolved into liquids; or burnt to ashes to be used in spells.

HOW TO MAKE PRAYER PAPERS

Hand writing out a portion of Scripture from the Bible produces a powerful form of prayer in text.

When we take the time to write out a Psalm, verse, or chapter from the Bible, we are making a link from our spirit to our hand and finally to the text we are writing. Prayer has its own weight, but added to this is the thought and effort you spent in composing the material or reciting it in your mind or aloud as you wrote out the paper, and the time your hands have spent conveying those conceptions to the prayer paper.

You do not need a special form of paper or ink. Over the years people have utilized every surface from the finest sheepskin parchment to cheap ruled copy-book pages, from torn shopping sacks to fine-grained cigarette papers. Write with a pencil, ink-pen, or marker, as suits your needs.

BURNING PRAYER PAPERS TO MAKE BIBLE ASHES

Prayer papers can be burnt to ashes in the flame of a candle, and by doing so the prayers are allowed to float upwards on the candle smoke.

Prayer papers can also be burnt on a bed of incense, either resin incense on charcoal or self-lighting powder incense, thus creating "Bible ashes" or "prayer ashes." The prayer or portion of Scripture becomes a part of the incense, and the ash from the burning contains the prayers as well as the herbs or resin from the incense.

Ash created in this way can be mixed with local dirt, graveyard dirt, sachet powders, powdered herbs, more incense powders, or sand, and depending upon what the ashes were mixed with, the resulting mixture can then be sprinkled around a piece of property, cooked into food, mixed with sachet powders for use in drawing altar designs, or used to line and insulate incense burners or candle trays.

BOILING OR INFUSING PRAYER PAPERS

Although we would never boil a Bible to extract its power into liquid, such acts were done in the past. We hear a tantalizing tale about such an event in Rev. Robert Hamill Nassau's *Fetichism in West Africa* from 1904: *"One day Dr. Good missed a Bible. It had been stolen. He heard nothing of it for a month; after which he was one day walking through a native village where the people, expecting to go to war the next day, were preparing a very powerful fetish or 'war medicine' by boiling together in a pot several of their most reliable fetishes; and in the boiling pot he found his Bible."*

Similar results can be obtained without desecrating a Bible by writing out a passage from Scripture and then boiling the prayer paper in plain water. This is traditionally done with water used for spiritual floor washes, baths, or rub-downs. Alternatively, when preparing a bath or floor wash, the text can be boiled with roots to make a decoction or steeped with herbs to make an infusion. The decoction or infusion is then strained for use.

BATHING, WASHING, AND LAUNDERING WITH PRAYERS

One powerful use for scriptural texts is their addition to baths, rub-downs, floor washes, or laundry water. To do this, you prepare either a liquid decoction or infusion, or Bible ashes, as described above. The liquid or ash is then added to the spiritual bath, rub-down preparation, floor wash, or laundry water, along with its other ingredients and prayed over. You can read more about these traditional forms of work in Aura Laforest's book *Hoodoo Spiritual Baths: Cleansing Conjure with Washes and Waters*.

Find Read

INGESTION OF INFUSED PRAYERS

A Bible verse written in ink can be soaked in water, whisky, wine, or beer, and the liquid can then be drunk. You may also add the paper to a magical herbal tea as you brew it. An older method is to use food colouring or berry juice to write out the Scripture onto a white plate. The Scripture is then rinsed off the plate with clean water into a glass and the verse literally drunk down. AIRR member Lukianos carries on this tradition with a spiritual rite he calls "Drink Your Sins, Drink Your Prayers."

Write your prayers
Drink your prayers

THE BIBLE STOPS A BULLET

"He shall cover thee with his feathers, and under his wings shalt thou trust: his truth shall be thy shield and buckler."
— Psalms 91:4

There are countless stories, both modern and antique, that tell of a soldier's life being saved when a breast-pocket Bible stopped the path of a fatal bullet. Here we see the value of the protective power of the Bible. A few examples drawn from narrative memoirs will illustrate the point.

- Civil War: *"The Bible was not only instrumental in saving souls: there are hundreds of cases where it was also instrumental in saving the lives of the soldiers. Here is a copy [holding it up] which was published in England by Messrs. Eyre and Spottiswoode. That Testament has a history which, if it could speak, I might well remain silent. It ran the blockade; it found its way to a soldier of the Southern army, who placed it in his bosom, and here is the hole which was made by a bullet, which, entering at the last chapter of the Revelation, penetrated through the first chapter of Matthew, and, grazing the outer cover, saved the man's life. There are hundreds of such copies preserved in numerous families throughout America, and money could not purchase them."* — *The Life of George H. Stuart* by George Hay Stuart.

- Civil War: *"Marse Tom was just wounded. If he hadn't had a Bible in his pocket de bullet go clear through his heart. But you all know no bullet ain't goin' through de Bible. No, you can't shoot through God's word."* — *When I Was a Slave: Memoirs from the Slave Narrative Collection* by Norman R. Yetman.

- World War II: *"William R. Wilson, a nineteen-year-old youth of New Castle, Pa., had a narrow escape from death while on duty in the American Army in France. A German sharpshooter fired at him so accurately that he would have been killed had it not been that a Bible in his left breast-pocket arrested the bullet sufficiently to cause only a slight wound."* — *Patriotic Illustrations for Public Speakers* by William Herbert Brown.

GIVE YOUR HERO GOD'S WEAPON

THIS AMAZING Bullet-Proof COVER CAN ACTUALLY SAVE HIS LIFE!

GENUINE MILITARY SIZE

BULLET-PROOF HEART-SHIELD BIBLE

THE ENGRAVED GOLD-PLATED, BULLET-PROOF FRONT COVER PROTECTS HIS HEART, SAVES LIVES!

NEW TESTAMENT OR CATHOLIC PRAYER BOOK EDITIONS

The Gold-Plated, 20-Gauge Bullet-Proof Steel Cover has been subjected to Target Tests. In Every Case 45-cal. Service Bullets shot at an Angle have been Deflected. It may as Miraculously Deflect Bayonets or Shrapnel.

$2.98

THIS GOLD-PLATED STEEL COVER WILL DEFLECT A 45-CAL. BULLET

The Ideal Gift for Son Husband Brother Sweetheart

Over 3½ million carried during World War II

Let God walk with your hero across the battlefield, providing him with guidance, filling his soul with courage and devotion toward God and country. Be sure he always carries a bullet-proof Heart-Shield Bible or Heart-Shield Catholic Prayer Book to protect his heart. It CAN SAVE HIS LIFE! Packed in a ready-to-mail carton. Order immediately for all of your loved ones.

SEND NO MONEY! Send name and address. Specify New Testament or Catholic Prayer Book. Pay postage on arrival plus C.O.D. fees. Send cash we pay all postage. Satisfaction guaranteed.

PROTECTO BIBLE CO.

Gold-plated, steel-covered, bullet-proof Heart-Shield Bibles were widely sold from World War I through the Vietnam War by makers such as the Protecto Bible Co. of Saint Louis, Missouri; the Know Your Bible Co. of Cincinnati, Ohio; and the Bible For Victory Co. of New York City. Their covers were stamped with a prayer-like motto such as, "May This Keep You Safe From Harm," "God's Weapon," or "May the Lord Be With You." During World War II many included a page from President Franklin D. Roosevelt in which he commended the Bible because, *"Throughout the centuries men of many faiths and diverse origins have found in the Sacred Book of words of wisdom, counsel and inspiration. It is a fountain of strength and now, as always, an aid in attaining the highest aspirations of the human soul."*

BIBLE AMULETS AND CHARMS

Portions of the Bible such as the 23rd Psalm, the Lord's Prayer, and the Ten Commandments are often displayed in Christian homes as porcelain plates, wall plaques, statuary, embroidered samplers, and framed prints. What is more surprising to those in some circles is that Jewish religious goods such as yads, shofars, menorahs, Sabbath and Havdalah candles, kosher salt and soap, and besamim spices have also been widely accepted in African-American hoodoo practice since the 1920s. First they were given English-language names: The yad became a "Holy Wand," the shofar a "Ceremonial Ram's Horn," the menorah a "Candelabra," and the Havdalah candle a "Multi-Wick Novelty Candle." By the 1930s, new, conjure-oriented attributions followed: According to occult shop ads, the shofar was used by "Mediums and Invocators" to summon "some Spirit, Demon, or Goblin from the beyond," dirt from the Mount of Olives in Israel was offered to "Hoodooists and Occultists" for "dressing and other magical purposes," and besamim spices were burned on charcoal as "Lucky Money Herb Mix."

MIZPAH: THE WATCHTOWER OF THE HEART

The first mizpah was an agreement between Jacob and his father-in-law Laban not to pass onto each other's land "to do evil." They erected a stone cairn as a sign of their oath, and although none but the two were present, still God had seen, for *"God is a witness between you and I."* Later the stone marker was built up to become a watchtower, also called a mizpah. In time, the word mizpah came to signify an emotional bond between those who are separated physically or by death, and was engraved onto headstones in graveyards and on other memorials.

Mizpah amulets most often take the form of a coin-shaped pendant. The charm is cut into two pieces by a zig-zag line, each of the pieces bearing part of the words of Genesis 31:49: *"The Lord watch between me and thee, when we are absent one from another."* One of the pieces is worn by each of the two people to signify their bond and to protect them while they are apart. First given by fathers to their sons going to war, they later became gifts shared by husbands and wives or sweethearts and best friends. The mizpah charm was first created as a Jewish talisman, but was very long ago absorbed into German-American and African-American Christian culture.

CRUCIFIX RINGS

Finger rings in the form of Christ crucified have been sold via hoodoo catalogues since the 1920s. They symbolize the sacrifice of Jesus, and thus bring protection through the shedding of His blood.

TEN COMMANDMENT CHARM BRACELETS

Ten Commandments charm bracelets consist of a regular metal-link charm bracelet with ten charms — one for each of the Commandments. Quite often the charms take the form of people acting out the principles of the individual Commandments, with Roman numerals to tell us which one is which. They serve as reminders of God's instructions to us.

BIBLE LOCKETS

Small pendants in the shape of a Bible held together by a clasp often open to display a small copy of the Lord's Prayer within. By inserting a picture of yourself and the one you love into the locket, the pictures are in front and the Lord's Prayer works protectively from behind

MIDGET BIBLES

Miniaturized books of Scripture, called "Midget" or "Mini" Bibles, are often sold for use as lucky key chain charms and may be placed inside a mojo bag along with appropriate herbs, roots, and other magical ingredients to form a powerful scriptural talisman in the hoodoo style.

LORD'S PRAYER AND TEN COMMANDMENT PENNIES

Rolled or elongated cents are regular United States coins that are fed into a metal rolling machine that flattens and lengthens them, while adding a new embossed design in place of the original minted image. Historically, the most popular of these coins are those bearing the Ten Commandments and the Lord's Prayer embossed into the copper in tiny type. While on the surface they appear to be little more than small novelties, in fact they are potentially powerful amulets when dressed with Holy Oil.

THE PROTECTIVE MEZUZAH

"And thou shalt write them upon the door posts of thine house, and upon thy gates."

— Deuteronomy 11:20

Scriptural text empowers the small rectangular boxes found on the doorposts of Jewish homes. These mezuzah talismans, although small, carry a big message; that holy words can protect and purify you. In Biblical times "mezuzah" simply meant the doorpost of a house.

- **Exodus 12:7; 22, 23:** The mezuzah was where the blood was applied at the first Passover.
- **Exodus 21:6:** A servant who wanted to serve his master for life had his ear pierced at the mezuzah.
- **1 Samuel 1:9:** Eli the Prophet sat by the mezuzah of the sanctuary.

Over time the meaning of the word mezuzah shifted from the doorpost to the box attached to it, and finally to the scroll in the box, inscribed with text from Deuteronomy 6:4-9 (*"And these words, which I command thee this day, shall be in thine heart [...] And thou shalt write them upon the posts of thy house, and on thy gates."*) and Deuteronomy 11:13-21. On the reverse of the scroll is a name of God, Shaddai (Almighty), an acronym for Shomer daltot Yisræl (Guardian of the Doors of Israel). Shin, the first letter of Shaddai, Shema, and Shomer daltot Yisræl, may decorate the mezuzah case.

In the 20th century, Jews freely shared the magic of the mezuzah with African-American root doctors. Mezuzahs were sold via ads in the *Chicago Defender,* and in the 1951 Clover Horn hoodoo catalogue from Baltimore, it was said that *"Many people carry the Hebrew Mazuzah as a good luck token to ward off evil and attract favourable vibrations. Each mazuzah contains sacred writings written on Parchment in a highly polished case."*

The folklore of the mezuzah parallels its religious significance. Jewish custom states that if you move, you should leave the mezuzah for the next occupant, so certain rental properties and homes have become desirable because of the mezuzot affixed to them. Some hold that a mezuzah repels evil; others say that a house lacking one is open to ill fortune; and today there are many who affix mezuzah charms to the doorposts of their cars.

SCRIPTURAL MAGIC

"Is not my word like fire, declares the Lord, and like a hammer that breaks the rock in pieces?"

— Jeremiah 23:29

For centuries people have used not just the Psalms but the entirety of the Holy Scriptures to bring about magic. Jewish kabbalists, and others after them, developed scriptural spells with verses from almost every book of the Bible. These magical uses of Scriptural verses have come down to us from the followers of Jewish, Christian, Spiritualist, and hoodoo practice.

The kabbalists attributed deep magical importance to certain portions of the Torah which they thought to be particularly efficacious. They felt that anyone who reads daily Exodus 16, the chapter about the manna, would be guarded against a lack of food and that a daily reading of Exodus 30:34-38, which details the composition of the Temple incense, would protect one against magic, evil spirits, and plagues, and that it could even delay death by warding off the Angel of Death.

The words of Holy Scripture are potent charms against the forces of evil. In times when spirit attacks are more likely, such as before a funeral, during the hours of childbirth, or in times of sickness or trouble, studying the Bible is believed to be a preventative aid against demonic forces. Simhah ben Samuel of Vitry, a French talmudist of the 11th-12th centuries, put it this way: *"As soon as a man has ceased his preoccupation with the words of Torah, Satan has permission to attack."*

Most useful of all of these is said to be the portion of the Bible which describes the sacrificial offerings. Regular study of these verses is believed to be an effective substitute for the actual sacrifices, and thus to bring about wondrous rewards, for, in the words of the 17th century Rabbi Abraham Horowitz, *"If people knew how important these verses are they would cherish each letter as though it were a crown of gold upon their head."*

Generally, the verses chosen for magical use are of two kinds: verses which, because they contain the name of God or speak of His power and acts have come to be regarded as being possessed of His innate power, and verses which seem to have a direct relationship and bearing on the current situation to be dealt with.

SELECTED SCRIPTURES FOR MAGICAL USE

There are so many Bible verses used for magical work that space prohibits us from sharing but a few. We have therefore chosen a short but potent selection of Scripture, listed in order from Genesis to Revelation:

- **Genesis 2:24:** To keep a man at home.
- **Genesis 37:1:** On entering a new home.
- **Genesis 49:18:** For protection at night.
- **Exodus 6:6-7:** For salvation from impending danger.
- **Exodus 14:14:** To help against a bully.
- **Exodus 36:8:** On beginning a piece of work.
- **Numbers 6:24-27:** To drive off demons and evil spirits.
- **Numbers 12:13:** To dispel a fever.
- **Numbers 21:17-20:** Against the evil eye.
- **Deuteronomy 18:13:** Against wild beasts.
- **Deuteronomy 21:10:** To be victorious in time of war.
- **Deuteronomy 33:3-4:** For intelligence.
- **Proverbs 1:26-28:** Against an enemy.
- **Proverbs 5:18-19:** To help a married man with impotency.
- **Proverbs 28:22:** To reverse back jealousy and the evil eye.
- **Isaiah 10:14:** For the financial ruin of an enemy.
- **Ezekiel 16:6:** To stop bleeding and heal small wounds.
- **Amos 2:13:** Against an oppressor.
- **Obadiah 1:6:** To find that which has been lost.
- **Habakkuk 2:2-3:** For aid in the development of automatic writing.
- **Habakkuk 2:15:** To stop a man from consorting with bad company.
- **Zechariah 4:13-14:** To learn who your teacher or guide is.
- **Mark 5:29:** To stop an unhealthy female discharge of blood.
- **Mark 16:18:** For protection against poisoning.
- **Luke 10:19:** Used to heal snake bite.
- **John 19:34-35:** For protection against injury and bleeding.
- **Ephesians 6:1:** To command obedience from unruly children.
- **2 Timothy 1:7:** To overcome fear, powerlessness, and mental anxiety.
- **Titus 1:12:** To overcome the wickedness of others.
- **Hebrews 13:4:** If one suspects marital infidelity.
- **Revelation 21:8:** Against people working magic on you.

7 BIBLE VERSES THAT SHOW GOD IS LISTENING
by Miss Michaele of HoodooPsychics.com

- **Psalms 18:2:** *"The Lord is my rock, and my fortress, and my deliverer; […] my buckler, […] my high tower."* Used to protect from robbers and also to recover from illness. Dress your doors and windows with oil in a five-spot pattern while reciting this. If you have been ill, do the same to your medicine cabinet.
- **Psalms 23:5:** *"Thou preparest a table before me in the presence of mine enemies: thou anointest my head with oil; my cup runneth over."* Recite this verse while grocery shopping and cooking. Make it part of your grace before meals. Remind yourself of it by printing out a copy of the Rider-Waite-Smith tarot card of the Ace of Pentacles.
- **Psalms 37:11:** *"But the meek shall inherit the earth; and shall delight themselves in the abundance of peace."* Used to banish evildoers and enemies. Write it out and place it under a white candle dressed with Blessing Oil and White Mustard Seed, along with your petitions for justice and good government.
- **Psalms 46:1-2:** *"God is our refuge and strength, a very present help in trouble. Therefore will not we fear, though the earth be removed, and though the mountains be carried into the midst of the sea."* In earthquake country or where vulnerable to landslides, write this out and place it in a small durable box attached to the foundation of your house. Can also be used to strengthen a troubled marriage.
- **Psalms 55:22:** *"Cast thy burden upon the Lord, and he shall sustain thee: he shall never suffer the righteous to be moved."* Write out the words *"Psalms 55:22"* on your money next time you buy groceries or pay for other necessities of life.
- **Matthew 11:28-30:** *"Come unto me, all ye that labour and are heavy laden, and I will give you rest […]."* Write this passage out in food colouring on a piece of paper and drop it into your next Uncrossing, Hyssop, or Van Van bath.
- **Revelation 21:3-4:** *"And I heard a great voice out of heaven saying […] And God shall wipe away all tears from their eyes; and there shall be no more death, neither sorrow, nor crying […]"* This is the capstone of God's promises, the ultimate blessed assurance that everything will be all right.

PLEADING THE BLOOD OF JESUS

> *"And he shall kill the lamb [...] and the priest shall take some of the blood [...] and put it upon the tip of the right ear of him that is to be cleansed, and upon the thumb of his right hand, and upon the great toe of his right foot."*
> —Leviticus 14:25

> *"And ye shall take a bunch of hyssop, and dip it in the blood [...] and strike the lintel and the two side posts with the blood."*
> —Exodus 12:22

> *"And they overcame him by the blood of the Lamb, and by the word of their testimony."*
> — Revelation 12:11

> *"...We have redemption through his blood ...."*
> — Ephesians 1: 7

The expression "pleading the blood of Jesus" is often heard amongst Christians, but, what exactly does it mean to plead the blood?

Simply put, this is the greatest of all Scriptural magics.

Just as the Israelites in Exodus 12:22 used hyssop herb to apply the blood of a lamb to their door posts to protect them from the Angel of Death, so do we plead the blood of Jesus Christ to turn back and stop the attacks of Satan. We do this with prayer, for *"the word of testimony"* (Revelation 12:11) is symbolic of the bunch of hyssop with which the Israelites marked their doorposts with the blood of the lamb, and, as Romans 10:10 tells us, *"With the the mouth confession is made unto salvation."* To merely know of the power in the blood is not sufficient. Speaking aloud is also necessary.

Any time you feel that the armies of darkness or spiritual attacks of any kind are coming against you, plead the blood of Jesus to protect you!

There is no one way to do this, for it is not a "formula." Use whatever words the Holy Spirit, your church training, or your own heart speaks:

"I rebuke all spirits of torment and fear through the blood of Jesus! Satan, I hold the blood of Jesus against you! I command you to stop in Jesus' name. The blood of Jesus redeems me! The blood of Jesus protects me! I plead the blood of Jesus over my home, my life, and my family! Amen."

PSALMIC MAGIC

"And he hath put a new song in my mouth..."
— Psalms 40:3

The Book of Psalms or Psaltery is a collection of 150 ancient Hebrew poems or songs. It forms one of the most beloved portions of the Bible, equally revered by Jews and Christians alike.

Many of the Psalms (called Tehilim in Hebrew) were written by the Jewish King David, who was himself a harpist. Seventy-three of the Psalms specifically bear the king's name as their author. Additionally, thirteen of the Psalms have headings that refer to events in David's life; these are Psalms 3, 7, 18, 34, 51, 52, 54, 56, 57, 59, 60, 63, and 142.

The tradition of praying the Psalms for help in magical, medical, or civil matters originated as an old Jewish custom. Over the centuries Jewish folk magicians, home practitioners, and kabbalists developed dozens of methods of working with the Psalms not only to pray, but also to assist in the consecration of talismans, the preparation of magical supplies, and the casting of spells for love, protection, safe travel, and business success.

In Jewish tradition, a Psalter may also be consulted in matters of divination. To divine with it you need to have a copy of the book — that is, a stand-alone Book of Psalms — and a moment of calm silence. Close your eyes, ask the question, open the book at random, and set your finger at the place on the page that feels correct in your heart. Then open your eyes and read the line that your finger touches. There is your answer!

It is said that if the Psalm your finger chose does not specifically answer your question, it may be that God is using that Psalm to warn you of upcoming danger, prepare you for an unexpected blessing, or otherwise lead you to a previously unseen path.

Perhaps the earliest written material on the use of Psalms in magic is the Hebrew text *Shimmush Tehilim (On the Use of the Psalms),* which dates back to the 10th century CE. In the 1700s Johannes Gottfried Seelig, a German Jewish convert to Christianity, translated *Shimmush Tehilim* into German. Later Seelig immigrated to the United States, bringing the book with him, and by the early 1800s, it was a well-accepted part of the Pennsylvania German Christian practice of braucherei folk magic, also known as Pow Wow magic.

SECRETS OF THE PSALMS

In the late 19th century, Seelig's German-language edition of *Shimmush Tehilim* was translated into English by the American Ashkenazi Jewish publishers the Wehman Brothers under the title *Secrets of the Psalms, A Fragment of the Practical Kabbalah,* now attributed to the highly anglicized name "Godfrey Selig."

The Wehman Brothers' inexpensive, popular English-language edition of this ancient Jewish book was soon introduced to the African-American folk magic community by Jewish drug store and occult shop owners. By the early 1900s, *Secrets of the Psalms* had become one of the most sought-after and frequently consulted books used by Christian conjure doctors and spiritual practitioners. In the 1930s it was kept in print hanks to the publishing efforts of Joseph Spitalnick (Joe Kay) and his family. Its reputation and vast popularity continue to this very day.

Secrets of the Psalms is divided into two sections. The first half of the book contains brief descriptions of the particular powers of each Psalm and ritual instructions for each Psalm's most effective use. The second half of the book is the full text of the King James Version of the Psalms.

The book draws upon what is known nowadays as "practical kabbalah," a branch of the Jewish mystical tradition that concerns the use of magic. These magical traditions come down from Talmudic times through to the Middle Ages. Esoteric and speculative concepts such as the occult kabbalistic Tree of Life will not be found here, but you will find instructions for making amulets, effectively reciting prayers, and simple spells, as well as which of the many mystical "Names of the Psalms" to speak or hold in mind as you do the work.

THE MYSTERIOUS "NAMES OF THE PSALMS"

In *Secrets of the Psalms* we see recommendations to "keep in mind the holy name", which varies from Psalm to Psalm. Some of these names resemble familiar archangelic names such as Gabriel (Strong Man of God), Raphael (Healer of God), and Michael (He Who is Like God). Others bear resemblances to the divine names of God in the Bible, such as Yahweh and Adonai. But what of such names as Sach, Paltioel, and El Sliyon?

Where did such exotic holy names come from?

DISCOVERING THE SACRED NAMES OF THE PSALMS

We have been told that the Scriptures just might be made up entirely of holy names so deeply embedded in the text that only the righteous can ever discover them all. There are many systems for uncovering these sacred names. They may be revealed by rearranging, recombining, substituting letters, splitting words into smaller groups, reading backwards, and many other variations. Joshua Trachtenberg's *Jewish Magic and Superstition* describes various methods for the generation of these sacred names, some of which we will attempt to summarize here:

- **Gematria** assigns a numerical value to each letter of the Hebrew alphabet. This method is easier for Hebrew speakers because each Hebrew letter possesses a numerical value. These sums are then compared to the sums of other words in an attempt to discover divine truth. For example, in Hebrew the Name of God and the words for "good" and "first" each add up to the number 17. This then is proof, if you need it, that God is "good" and "first" above all.
- **Notarikon** derives new words by using each of the initial or final Hebrew letters of a set of words to stand for another word, thus forming a type of acronym from the original words. Variations use the first and last letters or the two middle letters of a word in order to form another word. Notarikon is by no means restricted to magical use. For example, the Hebrew name of Maimonides — Rabbi Moshe ben Maimon — becomes "the RamBam," the name by which he is universally known throughout the Jewish world.
- **Temurah** involves the substitution of letters in certain words to create new words, meanings, or sacred names. The three basic forms of Temurah are:
    - **Avgad:** Replace each letter with the preceding letter:
    B = A, C = B, D = C, E = D.
    - **Atbash:** Replace the first letter with the last letter of the Hebrew alphabet, the second with the next-to-last, and so on:
    A = Z, B = Y, C = X, D = W.
    - **Albam:** Replace the first letter of the alphabet with the twelfth, the second with the thirteenth, and so on:
    A = L, B = M, C = N, D = O.

THE BOOK OF PSALMS IN FOLK MAGIC

One can, of course, sing the Psalms or Psalters, but in common Jewish, Protestant, Catholic, and Spiritualist traditions it is more usual to recite them, either from memory or from a book such as a *Tehillim*, Psalter, or Bible. Recitation of Psalms can be performed on its own as a type of prayer, but in folk magical practices, the recitation of Psalms often accompanies other acts of ritual endeavour, such as bathing, spiritually cleaning a home or business, perfuming a room with incense, suffumigating objects or people, placing candles or vigil lights upon an altar, or preparing a mojo bag.

The Jewish custom of reciting Psalms over oils or waters in order to fix or empower them for use in cooking or for use in cleansing or massage is also found in hoodoo and conjure practice.

It is also considered auspicious to recite daily the chapter of the Psalms that corresponds to the current year of one's life. For example, someone who is 20 years old should recite Chapter 21 of The Book of Psalms.

We provide for you here a short list of traditional psalms for special occasions. A lengthier index, sorted by Psalm number, follows.

- **To find a mate:** 32, 38, 70, 71, 72, 82, 121, 124
- **On the day of a wedding:** 19
- **For an end to infertility:** 102
- **For healthy childbirth:** 4, 5, 8, 20, 35, 57, 93, 108, 142
- **Upon the birth of a child:** 20,139
- **For recovery from illness:** 6, 13, 20, 22, 23, 30, 32, 38, 41, 51, 86
- **For livelihood:** 23, 34, 36, 62, 65, 67, 85, 104, 121,136, 144, 145
- **For peace:** 46
- **For divine guidance:** 139
- **For repentance:** 51, 90
- **For help in troublesome times:** 20, 38, 85, 86, 102, 130, 142
- **Prayer recited when travelling or in physical danger:** 91
- **Psalm of thanksgiving for a miracle:** 18
- **Psalm of thanksgiving upon being rescued:** 124
- **In a house of mourning:** 49
- **At a gravesite or on the anniversary of a death:** 33, 16, 17, 72, 91
- **At the dedication of a monument:** 1

Religious Goods in hoodoo catalogues, 1934 - 2014. Art by Charles C. Dawson, Charles M. Quinlan, and One Unknown Artist for Famous Products, Oracle Products, Clover Horn, Standard O & B Supply, and the Lucky Mojo Curio Company.

A QUICK LIST OF THE 150 PSALMS AND THEIR USES

Most old-time rootworkers and conjure doctors have at one time or another compiled comprehensive lists of the 150 Psalms with their magical attributions. Some have stuck slips of paper into their Bibles, identifying the various Psalms by use. No two lists will ever be the same, due to the nature of the oral history basis of folk magic, but some traditional lists have been published over time. The best-known of these is the list in Godfrey Selig's book *Secrets of the Psalms,* based on centuries-old Jewish sources.

The following list, a bit different from Selig's, was compiled through consultation with a number of professional root doctors. It comes to us courtesy of the Association of Independent Readers and Rootworkers and can be seen in full at the AIRR web site, where there are links to each individual Psalm, and more information about how each is used:

ReadersAndRootworkers.org/wiki/Category:The_Book_of_Psalms

Psalms 1: For removal of the ungodly from a group; for a safe pregnancy.
Psalms 2: To aid in disbanding and breaking up enemy conspiracies.
Psalms 3: For relief from a severe headache or from back pain.
Psalms 4: For restful and peaceful sleep; to change one's luck from bad to good.
Psalms 5: For finding favour with authorities or superiors in business.
Psalms 6: For healing diseases of the eye; for protection in the dark.
Psalms 7: To stop conspiracies, enemy pursuit, for court cases.
Psalms 8: Business success through the good will of associates; blessing of oils.
Psalms 9: To punish enemies; to restore health to male children; for court cases.
Psalms 10: To cleanse off an unclean, restless, or intranquil spirit.
Psalms 11: To cast off fear; for righteous retribution against your foes.
Psalms 12: For protection against severe persecution or oppression.
Psalms 13: For safety from unnatural death; for curing painful eye diseases.
Psalms 14: To stop libel and slander from tarnishing the trust others have in you.
Psalms 15: To exorcise evil spirits and devils from a person; for mental peace.
Psalms 16: To identify a thief; to change sorrow to joy and heal to pain.
Psalms 17: For safe travel abroad and to help bring a loved one safely home.
Psalms 18: To drive off approaching robbers; for anointing the sick to cure them.
Psalms 19: For help in childbirth, for release from jail, to remove evil spirits.
Psalms 20: Protection from danger for a day; to be justified in a court case.
Psalms 21: To both calm a storm and to offer protection for seafarers and sailors.
Psalms 22: For travel protection from dangerous storms, pirates, beasts, and men.
Psalms 23: For prosperity, love, protection, wisdom, and guidance.
Psalms 24: For protection from floods and escape from rising waters.

Psalms 25: Forgiveness of the sins of youth; protection from capture.
✷ Psalms 26: For the release of someone from confinement or from jail.
Psalms 27: For protection and hospitality while one is travelling abroad.
Psalms 28: To bring back estranged friends who have become hostile to you.
Psalms 29: To drive out devils and restore peace and tranquility to the home.
Psalms 30: For protection from enemies; for recovery from severe illnesses.
Psalms 31: For protection from conspiracies, back-biting, and gossip.
Psalms 32: To gain respect, love, grace, and blessings from Heaven.
Psalms 33: To protect, unite, and bless all of the members of a family.
Psalms 34: To destroy and reverse back evil; for protection while travelling.
Psalms 35: For justice to prevail in court cases and legal matters.
Psalms 36: For protection from slander and gossip and to expose liars.
Psalms 37: For protection against slander, gossip, lies, and evil-doers.
Psalms 38: To help in court cases where slander fouled up the proceedings.
Psalms 39: To turn around a court case when false testimony has been given.
Psalms 40: For protection against evil spirits and to cast them out.
Psalms 41: To restore a good name if slander and gossip have ruined a reputation.
Psalms 42: For spiritual guidance; for answers in dreams; for love reconciliation.
Psalms 43: To work against slander and wicked people; to turn back evil.
Psalms 44: To guard and protect against enemies, invading armies, or war.
Psalms 45: For peace between husband and wife; to calm an angry spouse.
Psalms 46: To help a struggling marriage; to soothe marital tensions.
Psalms 47: To gain favour from those in power; for mastery over people.
Psalms 48: To destroy hateful and envious enemies; to seize them with terror.
Psalms 49: To help heal and ease serious illnesses, diseases, and fevers.
Psalms 50: For healing; to overcome fevers and other forms of sickness.
Psalms 51: For cleansing and removing sin, especially after acts of revenge.
Psalms 52: To end all manner of gossip and calumny by poison-tongued people.
Psalms 53: To protect from enemies whose names are known or unknown.
Psalms 54: To give protection by reversing works of evil and malice.
Psalms 55: To call upon the Lord to bring down retribution against attackers.
Psalms 56: For intercession by the Almighty to remove temptation and bad habits.
Psalms 57: To turn around one's luck, changing bad luck into good luck.
Psalms 58: For warding off snakes and wild beasts; to reverse evil unto enemies.
Psalms 59: To bring down the vengeance of the Lord against one's enemies.
Psalms 60: For the Lord to march into battle and protect His soldiers.
Psalms 61: For a new home to be fixed with good fortune, happiness, and peace.
Psalms 62: For forgiveness of sins and to gain the blessing of the Lord.
Psalms 63: To protect from being victimized by business partners and investors.
Psalms 64: For protection, especially while at sea, and for a safe return.
Psalms 65: For road opening that breaks through barriers and leads to success.
Psalms 66: To remove evil spirits; to heal those possessed; for wishes to come true.

Psalms 67: Against illness and fever; to free one who has been imprisoned or bound.
Psalms 68: Recited while preparing baths that are used to exorcise evil spirits.
Psalms 69: To free one from slavery to addictions and unhealthy habits.
Psalms 70: To cast down and reverse the wickedness wrought by enemies.
Psalms 71: To release clients from prison, for acquittals in court cases.
Psalms 72: To craft charms and talismans which bring a client favour and grace.
Psalms 73: To protect travelers against religious persecution in foreign lands.
Psalms 74: For an end to persecution and to destroy oppressors and persecutors.
Psalms 75: Used along with specially prepared baths for the cleansing of sins.
Psalms 76: For the Lord's intercession, to provide protection from all attacks.
Psalms 77: Used against danger, poverty, chronic illness, drought, and famine.
Psalms 78: To gain favours from kings, princes, and other government officials.
Psalms 79: To utterly destroy the wicked and also to cast fatal curses.
Psalms 80: To end spiritual doubts and to prevent people falling into unbelief.
Psalms 81: To save people from error and mistakes, for safety from accidents.
Psalms 82: To facilitate business deals and assist those making investments.
Psalms 83: To keep clients safe during times of war, persecution, and captivity.
Psalms 84: For healing, especially when the body has contracted unusual odours.
Psalms 85: To soften hearts and restore peace to friends who have become enemies.
Psalms 86: To bring goodness, spiritual peace, and happiness to the community.
Psalms 87: To cleanse the community before starting healing and blessing work.
Psalms 88: To remove evil and bring blessings; used with baths and talismans.
Psalms 89: Prayed over oil to anoint the sick or secure a release from prison.
Psalms 90: Used with Psalms 91 for protection; also to bless the work of the hands.
Psalms 91: For protection from distress and harm; to exorcise evil spirits.
Psalms 92: Prayed over herbal baths used to bring good fortune and high honours.
Psalms 93: Against prosecution by unjust and oppressive men; to win in court.
Psalms 94: For protection and to turn all evil back onto your enemies.
Psalms 95: To cleanse sins; to pray for guidance and forgiveness for enemies.
Psalms 96: To bless a family and bring happiness, peace, and joy to them.
Psalms 97: Used with Psalms 96 for healing, blessing, and cleansing a family.
Psalms 98: To restore peace between two hostile families; to bless a home.
Psalms 99: For praise and devotion to God; to gain conversation with God.
Psalms 100: To bring victory against enemies by uplifting the client.
Psalms 101: For protection against enemies and to be rid of evil spirits.
Psalms 102: For assistance in matters of fertility and to be granted grace.
Psalms 103: For help in conceiving of a child and for the forgiveness of sins.
Psalms 104: To cleanse away evil; to bless natural curios and spiritual supplies.
Psalms 105: For healing illnesses, especially recurrent or periodic fevers.
Psalms 106: For healing and to restore one to health, especially from fevers.
Psalms 107: For remission or healing from periodic or recurrent fevers.
Psalms 108: Utilized in a spell for financial success in your place of business.

Psalms 109: Used in a powerful curse against oppressive, slanderous enemies.
Psalms 110: For victory; to cause enemies to bow before you and beg for mercy.
Psalms 111: Recited to acquire many friends, as well as respect, and admiration.
Psalms 112: To increase in might and power, for success, abundance, and blessings.
Psalms 113: Prayers and blessings for those in need; to stop infidelity and heresy.
Psalms 114: Used in a spell for success in matters of finance, business, and money.
Psalms 115: To foster truth-telling, for victory in debate over scoffers and mockers.
Psalms 116: Recited daily for protection from violent or sudden death or injury.
Psalms 117: For forgiveness of a failure to keep a vow or promise that you made.
Psalms 118: For protection against those who try to misguide or lead you astray.
Psalms 119: The longest Psalm, its 22 alphabetic divisions cover all human problems.
Psalms 120: For success in court and for protection against snakes and scorpions.
Psalms 121: For safety at night; both during sleep and while travelling in darkness.
Psalms 122: For peace within a city, and to gain the favour of those in high station.
Psalms 123: Employed in a spell to cause a servant, trainee, or employee to return.
Psalms 124: Cleansing of the soul, protection at sea and from being wronged.
Psalms 125: For protection in foreign lands and against those who work iniquity.
Psalms 126: After miscarriage or the death of a child; for the next child to live.
Psalms 127: Placed in a mojo for the protection and blessing of a newborn baby.
Psalms 128: For a fortunate, accident-free pregnancy; for uncomplicated childbirth.
Psalms 129: Recited daily to prepare one for a long life of virtue and good works.
Psalms 130: Recited to the four quarters when passing by sentries in a war zone.
Psalms 131: Recited three times a day to reduce one's sin of pride and scornfulness.
Psalms 132: To remediate one's unpunctuality and failure to perform duties on time.
Psalms 133: To retain the love and respect of friends and to gain many more friends.
Psalms 134: For altar work in matters of higher education and for success in school.
Psalms 135: For repentance, spirituality, and rededication of one's life to God.
Psalms 136: Recited on behalf of those who wish to confess and be cleansed of sins.
Psalms 137: For cleansing of the heart and soul from hate, envy, evil, and vice.
Psalms 138: Recited daily to bring love and friendship from the Lord.
Psalms 139: To nurture and maintain love, especially within the context of marriage.
Psalms 140: To restore tranquility and to preserve and maintain relationships.
Psalms 141: To ward off against terror and fear and against looming oppression.
Psalms 142: To heal the body, restore health, and alleviate pain and suffering.
Psalms 143: To heal bodily limbs, especially the arms and to alleviate pain.
Psalms 144: To speed up healing and to ensure the perfect mend of a broken arm.
Psalms 145: To cleanse and purify clients who are beset by ghosts or evil spirits.
Psalms 146: Used with altar work for healing and recovery after being wounded.
Psalms 147: For healing wounds and bites from snakes, insects, and other animals.
Psalms 148: Used with Psalms 149 to keep clients safe from accidents by fire.
Psalms 149: Used with altar work to protect against fire-related accidents.
Psalms 150: For the glory of the Lord and to give thanks for His intervention.

YOU CAN DO ANYTHING WITH PSALMS 23

Psalms 23 is possibly the best-known Psalm in the world. It covers all the needs of life, and so it is often recommended for virtually any situation, including prosperity, love, protection, guidance, and even true dreams. Here are but a few of the spells that use this powerful and potent Psalm. There are more to be found under the various conditions.

PSALMS 23: AN OLD FASHIONED SPELL FOR PROTECTION
To protect yourself or others, burn a white candle while reciting the 23rd Psalm three times, either in your name or the name of another.

PSALMS 23: A PHOTOGRAPH AND OLIVE OIL LOVE SPELL
An old time worker from Waycross, Georgia reports that if you want someone to love you, take a picture of the person and put nine drops of Olive oil on the picture around the head. Then carry that picture in your pocket for nine days. For each of the nine days recite the 23rd Psalm over the picture and that will make the person care for you.

PSALMS 23: RETURN TO ME PHOTOGRAPH SPELL
Another conjurer of Waycross, Georgia advises that you can take two photographs, one of yourself and one of the person you wish to draw back to you. Write the 23rd Psalm on the back of one and the 42nd Psalm on the back of the other. Place them face to face under your pillow and sleep with them there. They will shortly return.

PSALMS 23: MISS CAT'S BAD LUCK REVERSAL SPELL
If you have broken a mirror and are facing seven years of bad luck, bury the pieces of the mirror in your back yard. Do not throw them away. Clean the area where the mirror broke with Chinese Floor Wash and then take a ritual bath for uncrossing or luck-changing while reciting the 23rd Psalm.

PSALMS 23: SANCTIFIED WATER
To make Sanctified Water, which is used just as Holy Water is, you pray Psalms 23 over a container of water. You can add a pinch of salt or a couple of drops of Rose Oil to give the water a bit more pep.

PSALMS 23: OLD TIME BLESSED OLIVE OIL

There are many ways to prepare blessed Olive oil; this is one of several traditional methods. On a Sunday while the hands of the clock are rising, pour Olive oil into a large bowl and sprinkle a pinch of kosher salt into it. Then take a white cloth and place it over your head so that it covers both you and the bowl of Olive oil. When you are covered, bring the bowl near to your lips and pray Psalms 23 over the oil in such a way that your breath falls across it. When you finish the Psalm, remove the white cloth, cover the bowl with it, and place the covered bowl in a dark place. Repeat this for a total of seven days. After the seventh day bottle the now-blessed oil and keep it in a cool place to use. The oil may be used in healing or blessing rites or as a base for making scented oils.

PSALMS 23: A FAMOUS WISHING RITE WITH JOB'S TEARS

Make a sincere wish over seven Job's Tears seeds, then place them in your pocket and carry them this way for seven days. At the end of the seventh day, go to a place where there is running water. Recite aloud the 23rd Psalm, pray for your desire, and turn your back to the water. Throw the Job's Tears over your left shoulder into the water and walk away without looking back. In seven days, it is said, your wish will come true.

PSALMS 23: MAMA MICKI'S HEAD BLESSING PROTECTION

For blessings and to protect yourself, take a few drops of 7-11 Holy Oil and dress your hair or the crown of your head. While applying the oil say Psalms 23:5, *"Thou preparest a table before me in the presence of mine enemies; thou anointest my head with oil; my cup runneth over"* aloud.

PSALMS 23: TWENTY THREE DOLLAR BLESSING MIRACLE

Take 23 one-dollar bills and dress each of them with Blessing Oil in the five spot pattern while saying the 23rd Psalm aloud over each bill. Then take the dressed bills and donate them all to a worthy charity. After you have donated the money say Psalms 23:6 *"Lord, you have said, 'Surely goodness and mercy shall follow me all the days of my life: and I will dwell in the house of the Lord for ever.' I am believing in you for this favour [state your request]."* Do this daily for 23 days straight (that's a total of $529.00 you will donate to charity, in case you were wondering), and then leave the matter alone, as it is now in God's hands.

THE "CHICAGO PSALMS"

The "Chicago Psalms" are a series of four Psalms recommended by Morton Neumann from the early 1930s through the late 1970s. Neumann, a Jewish-American perfumer and chemist from Chicago, was at one time the major distributor of African-American cosmetics and conjure curios. His Morton Products, Valmor Beauty Supplies, Sweet Georgia Brown and Madame Jones cosmetics, and King Novelty goods were sold via his Famous Products Distribution network in hoodoo drug stores, via a system of agents who lived in the South, and by direct mail order through vividly graphic ads in the black-owned and nationally-distributed *Chicago Defender* and Philadelphia Courier newspapers.

Here are the Chicago Psalms of Morton Neumann, first published in 1934, complete with his unique system of capitalization:

THE BIBLE SAYS, "BURN INCENSE"

Frankincense resin is sometimes Burned by people while engaging in Spiritual Rites and Singing of Psalms. They feel that when they pray and meditate in its sweet fragrance, their Prayers are Answered Better. Some people believe that the burning of Incense Drives Away Evil and invites Lady Luck to smile upon them. One book mentions that in the year 1512 in the Mozarabic rite, Incense was used plainly as a sacrifice for the Appeasement of God's Wrath. Many of our customers like to Burn Incense and offer Prayer at the same time. Some of our customers have burned this Incense and read at different times Psalms 4, 8, 10, and 26. If you wish to use this method of Praying and at the same time Burn Frankincense Resin on Charcoal, you may of course turn to the Bible and read any Psalm that you wish or cite any Prayer that you should Desire.

PSALMS AGAINST EVIL SPIRITS

Psalms 10: If anyone believes they are plagued with an unknown or Evil Spirit they may Burn Frankincense Resin on Charcoal and pronounce, while burning, Psalms 10, keeping constantly in mind the Adorable name of God. Many people repeat, if they wish, the prayer which follows: *"O Lord, God, please break the power of this Evil, Obsessing Spirit, and Free me from his plagues and oppression. Wilt Thou strengthen me in Soul and Body and Deliver me from Evil Unclean Spirits? Amen."*

PSALMS FOR THOSE WHO HAVE BEEN UNLUCKY

Psalms 4: If you have heretofore been unfortunate or unlucky in spite of every effort, you can, if you wish, Burn Frankincense Resin on Charcoal while citing in a Prayerful manner Psalms 4 before Sunrise or in the morning with humility and devotion. Let your mind be uplifted in a true faith ever trusting in the Love of the Almighty God without whose assistance all must Perish. You may, if you wish, also repeat the Psalm which follows: *"May it please Thee, O God to Prosper my ways, steps and doings? Grant that my desires may be amply fulfilled and let my wishes be satisfied for the sake of the Thy Great, Mighty, and Praiseworthy Name. Amen."*

PSALMS FOR LOVE AND GOOD WILL OF ALL MEN

Psalms 8: Many people who desire the Love and Good-Will of all Men and Women in their Business, Financial, and Social Transactions or any other Matters, May if they wish, Burn Frankincense Resin on Charcoal while citing in a Prayerful Manner Psalms 8, all the while thinking of the Lord God, who has made Thee to have a Domain over the Works of Thy Hands. After citing this Prayer as given above, you may wish to cite the following Prayer: *"O Lord Almighty, may it please Thee to grant that I may obtain Love, and the Good Will of all Men and all Women in the transaction of my Business? I, at all times, promise Thee that I will be Honest and Straightforward in all my dealings according to Thy Holy Will. Amen."*

PSALMS FOR SUCCESS

Psalms 26: Many people who have been followed by Bad Luck or Misfortune and have been Unsuccessful in their Undertakings or have not been able to save Money, may, if they wish, Burn Frankincense Resin on Charcoal and cite Psalms 26 early every morning and late every evening. However, it is said they must have undivided faith in the Great and Unlimited Power of God to overcome all things and to help them so that their wishes may be fulfilled and so they may have plenty for themselves and their Loved Ones.

Neumann sold his own brand of Genuine Frank-Incense Compound, but these Psalms will work just as well with any good spiritual incense.

7 DEADLY BIBLE PSALMS TO QUELL YOUR FOES
by catherine yronwode of HoodooPsychics.com

Even religious people have enemies, suffer oppression, and need relief from cruelty. God has inspired some very serious prayers in the form of Psalms which can be recited while casting justified curses. Known as the "imprecatory Psalms," these prayers are powerful, effective, and definitely not to be trifled with!

- **Psalms 1:** *"The ungodly [...] are like the chaff which the wind driveth away [...] the way of the ungodly shall perish."* This Psalm removes unworthy and ungodly people from any group.
- **Psalms 37:** *"The arms of the wicked shall be broken [...] their sword shall enter into their own heart [and] the wicked shall perish [...] as the fat of lambs, [...] into smoke shall they consume away."* This cursing Psalm invokes physical injury and brings death by sword and fire to evil people.
- **Psalms 55:15:** *"Let death take my enemies by surprise; let them go down alive to the grave."* Here is a simple, direct, and right-to-the-point destruction Psalm. What's more, it asks God to give your enemies no warning, but to kill them unawares.
- **Psalms 58:6:** *"O God, break the teeth in their mouths."* Talk about specialized curses! This Psalm sends your enemies, especially gossipers, liars, and false tale-bearers, directly to the dentist!
- **Psalms 59:12:** *"For the sin of their mouth and the words of their lips let them be taken in their pride: and for cursing and lying which they speak."* God really hates liars, and this Psalm asks for particular curses to fall upon those who spread falsehoods or with arrogance or pride, or use foul language.
- **Psalms 109:8:** *"Let his days be few; and let another take his office."* Do you need to remove a bad politician or government official from your life? This is the Psalm to do it!
- **Psalms 137:9:** *"How blessed will be the one who seizes your infants and dashes them against the rocks!"* Finally, here is a terrible curse of vengeance that draws down God's ire upon entire families and employs military means to do so. Be careful with this one, folks — it's scary!

8 POWERFUL PSALMS TO REVERSE AND SEND BACK EVIL

These Psalms were written in times when the Israelites suffered crushing defeats and unspeakable atrocities; when they had been stripped of all support except for God. They are cited to call down a justified reversal of evil to the sender, typically while burning a Reversing or Double Action candle, crafting a mirror box, or singeing a doll or name paper in flame. These are serious Psalms. They should never be employed lightly or in a frivolous matter, but with faith in the justified power of the Lord.

- **Psalms 6:** *"Let all mine enemies be ashamed and sore vexed: let them return and be ashamed suddenly."*
- **Psalms 11:** *"Upon the wicked he shall rain snares, fire, and brimstone, and an horrible tempest: this shall be the portion of their cup."*
- **Psalms 12:** *"For the oppression of the poor, for the sighing of the needy, now will I arise, saith the Lord; I will set him in safety from him that puffeth at him."*
- **Psalms 40:** *"Let them be ashamed and confounded together that seek after my soul to destroy it; let them be driven backward and put to shame that wish me evil."*
- **Psalms 52:** *"God shall likewise destroy thee for ever, he shall take thee away, and pluck thee out of thy dwelling place, and root thee out of the land of the living."*
- **Psalms 54:** *"For strangers are risen up against me, and oppressors seek after my soul: they have not set God before them. Behold, God is mine helper: the Lord is with them that uphold my soul. He shall reward evil unto mine enemies: cut them off in thy truth."*
- **Psalms 69:** *"Let their table become a snare before them: and that which should have been for their welfare, let it become a trap."*
- **Psalms 79:** *"Pour out thy wrath upon the heathen that have not known thee, and upon the kingdoms that have not called upon thy name."*

After reciting Psalms of this gravity, it is important to seek God's forgiveness in case you have unjustly cursed an innocent person. Bathe, or at least wash your face and hands, with clean water to which you added Hyssop herb bath tea, Hyssop Oil, or Hyssop Bath Crystals, while you recite Psalms 51 *("Purge me with Hyssop...").* You may also drink Hyssop tea.

DIVINATORY MAGIC

"And ye shall know the truth, and the truth shall make you free."
— John 8:32

Bibliomancy means "divination by means of a book" — and among Jews and Christians the most popular book for use in divination is the Holy Bible. Because it is God's Holy Word it can provide a direct link to Spirit. It is the custom of most hoodoo root doctors to keep the Bible or The Book of Psalms on or near their altars at all times, and many workers consult the Bible for guidance or answers to questions.

BIBLIOMANTIC CLEIDOMANCY

Cleidomancy is "divination by means of a key." In cleidomancy proper, only a key is used, generally a skeleton key. The key is typically suspended by a ribbon or thread and consulted as one does with a pendulum for answering yes-or-no questions.

In Bibliomantic cleidomancy the skeleton key is combined with the Bible, as no other book is deemed suitable to this form of working.

One uses this method to discover the name of a thief, an enemy conjure doctor, or a wrong-doer of any kind. A large, old-fashioned skeleton key is inserted into a Bible with the top loop of the key protruding from the top of the pages. The Bible is closed and tightly wrapped with black silk ribbon. The portion of the key which protrudes is grasped, often by two people, each using only their little fingers to support the key. Children are deemed to be especially good at this, as their fingers are small and their hearts are pure.

With the Bible suspended by the key the names of the suspects are then slowly recited, full names being given where possible. When the guilty party's name is called the Bible will react. It may turn on the key, drop from the holders' fingers, or the key may slide out of the Bible. The name spoken when the Bible reacts is the guilty party.

If no reaction is found, the names are read again, just as slowly as the first time, and even a third time, if needed. If the Bible makes no response at all, even after three readings of the suspects' names, the method is set aside, and it is said that "God gave no signs" in this case.

BIBLICAL BIBLIOMANCY

The original practitioners of Biblical Bibliomancy were the Jews. Back when Tanakhs were hand-lettered scrolls and copies were not kept in the home, the custom arose that individuals weighing an important matter would go by a synagogue or Hebrew school to hear the children read aloud the daily portion of their Scripture studies. Whatever portion the listener heard was the one he or she was meant to hear. This method of aural bibliomancy was used by European Jews during the Middle Ages, and possibly earlier, and it is still used to this day.

Later, when printed, leaf-bound books became common, household Bibles, Books of the Psalms, and heavily ornamented Family Bibles containing the birth and death dates of ancestors and relatives became treasured heirlooms, and their efficacy as divinatory tools was widely endorsed in popular culture. Consulting the old Family Bible for guidance remains a potent form of divination among Jews and Christians to this day.

Please remember that the Bible is a sacred book, and it should always be used with reverence and respect. Frivolous questions are discouraged.

To begin a divination first you may say a short prayer, either silently or aloud. Then ask clear question, again either silently or aloud. Next, open the Bible at random. Many people open the Bible not once but three times, either for "The Father, Son, and Holy Ghost," or because "the third time is a charm." Some keep their eyes closed while the Bible is opened. No matter how you do it, once your page is selected, you move your index finger over the page in slow circles or figure eights until Spirit indicates to stop. Open your eyes and read the selected portion.

In general if the verse you selected is positive, the answer is seen as positive, and if the verse is negative, the answer is in the negative.

For example let's take the question "Will So-and-So marry me?"

The selection of I Samuel 26:13, *"Then David went over to the other side, and stood on the top of an hill afar off; a great space being between them"* would indicate increased distance, and thus an answer of "no."

Conversely, a selection of Judges 18:6, *"And the priest said unto them, Go in peace: before the LORD is your way wherein ye go"* would indicate a church wedding, a peaceful marriage, and thus an answer of "yes."

If Psalms 66:19: *"Verily God hath heard me; he hath attended to the voice of my prayer"* comes up, you've hit the jackpot: Your wishes will be granted.

DREAM BOOKS AND THE BIBLE

"Hear, I pray you, this dream which I have dreamed."
— Genesis 37:6

Dreams come to many in the Bible: Jacob, Joseph, Solomon, even Pharaoh. While we sleep God sends us messages and warnings. His ministering angels watch over us and whisper divine truths in our ears.

It is said, "a dream unexamined is like a letter unopened," and the Bible actually tells us how to open that unopened letter, in Habakkuk 2:2-3: *"And the Lord answered me, and said, Write the vision, and make it plain upon tables, that he may run that readeth it. For the vision is yet for an appointed time, but at the end it shall speak, and not lie: though it tarry, wait for it; because it will surely come, it will not tarry."*

In other words, dreamed prophesies, warnings, and tips are gifts from God. After waking up, first say a prayer of thanks for receiving your dream and then write it down on a sheet of clean paper so that it can later be understood and acted upon. If the images are unclear to you, the dream can be deciphered with the help of a dream book.

Dream books consist of alphabetical lists of dream images with short explanations, fortunes, and sets of lucky numbers for gaming. Long embedded in the hoodoo tradition, they provide a key to the meanings of dreams and an aid in betting. The many songs written about dream books by 20th century black blues musicians are a powerful indicator of their value as essential tools of contemporary rootwork. One of the most popular of these titles, the *Pick 'Em Dream Book*, written in 1954 by the famed African-American occult shop owner Rajah Rabo (Carl Z. Talbot, Jr., 1890-1974), clearly addresses dreams of the Bible and church:

- To dream of the Bible: *"Signifies that your religious teachings will unlock the door of understanding."*
- To dream of a church: *"Signifies that you should seek spiritual guidance, and it will help you to renew your faith in something [in] which you seem to have lost confidence."*

The *Pick 'Em Dream Book* not only includes meanings and numbers to bet for Catholic, Jewish, and Baptist churches, but also Church On Fire!

DEVOTIONAL MAGIC

A PRACTICAL GUIDE TO PRAYER

In *The Art of Hoodoo Candle Magic in Rootwork, Conjure, and Spiritual Church Services,* Rev. catherine yronwode describes eight types of prayer:
• **Prayerful Recital of Scriptures:** *"Those who are well versed in scriptural prayer may prescribe supplicatory or intercessory passages of the Bible that they deem most beneficial to the client's case."*
• **Prayer With Recitation of the Psalms:** *"Certain Psalms are prescribed for specific situations, either from memory or from a book."*
• **Supplicatory Prayer:** *"Prayers of supplication are also known as petitionary prayers; they are often simply called petitions."*
• **Intercessory Prayer:** *"A spiritual practitioner, deacon, minister, bishop, or group of people prays on behalf of others, to intercede for them with God."*
• **Imprecatory prayer:** *"The angry Psalms are very powerful prayers of vengeance, if spoken with conviction."*
• **Extemporaneous Prayer:** *"A prayer that is spoken or sung from the heart […] may combine concepts or wording borrowed from or inspired by Scriptures, Psalms, published prayers, or gospel songs."*
• **Affirmative Prayer:** *"A form of prayer or metaphysical technique that is focused on positive outcomes rather than negative situations."*
• **Prayer Chains:** *"In church usage, […] a loose confederation of people who agree to freely pray for one another."*

HOW SHALL WE PRAY?

In *The Magic Formula for Successful Prayer,* published in 1942, Mikhail Strabo presented a clear outline of Affirmative Prayer:
"When you ask God to do something for you, you must believe that it is an already accomplished fact. By accepting the accomplishment of your wish, affirmatively, you are helping God make it a reality.

"Think that He is actually doing the things that you have asked Him to do. Pray with the thoughts that the things you want are already yours, since time had begun. This, thinking with God, will make your prayers realities.

"That is the message that God has for you. These are the answers to your prayers. And that is the answer to the question: 'How to Pray?'"

PREACHING AS PRAYER

"And he said unto them, Go ye into all the world, and preach the gospel to every creature."

— Mark 16:15

We share with you now a form of traditional, public, congregational prayer. Its roots are old and it still thrives in the modern day. In form it is as much based in African poetic traditions as it is in the Bible. It is called "The Deacon's Prayer" because in black Protestant churches, this portion of the Sunday service is given over to the Deacons, trusted men of mature years who speak for and about the community.

THE DEACON'S PRAYER

There is no one way to say the Deacon's Prayer. It is not a recitation but a free-form, improvised call from the heart, incorporating several set pieces of wording. The phrases in italics below are samples only. If you don't already know this prayer, we suggest that you attend an old-school Baptist church or search YouTube for "The Deacon's Prayer" and watch until you understand this prayer's tone, tempo, melody, cadence, and gesture.

Thank You, Lord

Thank you, Lord, for waking me up this morning. You didn't have to do it, but you did. You gave me food to eat; I thank you, Lord. You gave me water to drink; I thank you Lord.

Everything that keeps you alive all day long is something to be thankful for. Every breath is a gift, a miracle, and a wonder.

Thank You for the Church

Thank you, Lord, for letting me come to church today. Thank you, Lord, for letting me greet my brethern and sisters here today. Lord we come together to uphold your name in praise today. We serve a mighty God.

The Deacon thanks God for the journey to church and rejoices in the presence of friends, family, and fellow congregants.

I Know Who You Are

Lord, I know that you're a midnight rider. I know that you're a doctor in the sickroom, Lord. I know that you're a lawyer in the courtroom.
Lord, we thank you, Jesus, for what you did for us on Calvary's cross. You been a mother for the motherless. You been a father for the fatherless. You are a bridge over troubled water, a rock in a weary land, Lord.
I know who you are, Lord; I know you're the same God that turned water into wine. I know you're able. I know who holds my hand. I know where my help comes from. I know I can depend on you, Lord.

The Deacon praises God's mighty power and steadfastness.

Now, Lord ...

Now, Lord, I come before you with bowed-down head and humble heart, thanking you, Jesus, for one more chance to pray.
Lord, I realize that someone has eyes, and they cannot see. Someone has legs, and they can't even walk, Lord. But right now, Jesus, I want you to go by the nursing home, Lord. I want you to stop by the jailhouse, Jesus.
Lord, someone far from home right now and he ain't got the fare. Lord, some mother praying for her son right now, and he's out on the street where he should not be. Lord, Jesus, we need your help right now. We ask you, Lord, to show your mercy, Lord, to those in need, in Jesus' name, Lord.

At this point the Deacon might pray for someone in the church who is in a bad situation, without mentioning names.

Thanks for Protection and Salvation

I thank you, Lord, that the sheets I covered up in were not my winding sheets. I thank you, Lord, that the bed I slept in was not my cooling board.
And I know that the devil can't do me no harm, for I got everything I need when I found Jesus. I may not see tomorrow, but I know who holds tomorrow in his hands.
You been mighty good to us, Lord. And we want you to give us a place in your kingdom, Lord, where we can praise your name forevermore.
In Jesus' name, Amen.

The Deacon places the prayer into a theological context of salvation.

A CURSE IN A BAPTIST SERMON: HITLER AND HELL

Hitler and Hell is a curse on Adolf Hitler in the form of a sermon that was recorded during World War Two by the renowned African-American preacher Rev. J. M. Gates. The curse is chanted in a Baptist sermon cadence, a capella, call-and-response style. Gates is accompanied by two parishioners, an alto woman and a bass man; their responses are timed together but are independent of one another. The use of rhythmical pauses allows the congregants to respond and amplify the commanding power of the text. We hope that you may glean from it the force and majesty of a true Christian sermon of imprecation preached by an anointed pastor. Our thanks go out to catherine yronwode for the detailed transcription of this text, which is online at LuckyMojo.com/hitler-and-hell.html —

HITLER AND HELL BY REV. J. M. GATES

Rev. Gates	Woman	Man
I want to speak to you	(Yeah)	
This morning	(All right)	(Well)
From this subject:	(Yes)	(Well)
Hitler	(Yes)	(Well)
And Hell	(Oh, yes)	(Glory!)
And when I speak	(Yes)	(Well)
And sing	(Yes)	(Well)
About Hitler	(Yes, sir)	(Well)
I can't help	(Yeah?)	(Tell us about it!)
But thinkin about Hell	(Yes)	(Well)
Hitler	(Oh, yes)	(Hallelujah!)
And Hell	(Oh, yes!)	(And Hell!)
They tell me	(Well)	(Well)
That he's a man	(Well, yes)	(Well)
Who lives	(Yes)	(Lives)

In a storm [cellar]	(Oh, yes)	(Well)
And has	(Yes, sir)	(Talk about it!)
His elevator	(Yes, sir)	(Well)
Service	(Yeah)	(Yeah)
To go	(Yeah)	(Yeah)
From one	(Oh, yeah)	(Yeah)
Station	(Yes, sir)	(Glory!)
To another	(Oh, yes)	(Hallellujah!)
In his town	(Oh, Lord)	(Now)
Now, I'm tellin you	(Oh, Lord)	(Pull up there!)
This mornin	(Yes, sir)	(Well)
That he	(Yes, sir)	(Hallellujah!)
Is the dictator	(Oh, yeah)	(Well)
Of Germany	(Yes, sir)	(Well)
Hitler,	(Oh, you!)	(Well)
You must come down!	(Oh, yes!)	(Must come down!)
You must come down!	(Yes)	(Well)
I'm saying to you	(Yes)	(Well)
As you	(Mmm-mmm)	(Glory!)
Sit back	(Oh, Lord)	(Hallelujah!)
In your easy chair	(Yes, God!)	(Well)
While men	(Yeah)	(Well)
Is dyin	(Yes, sir!)	(Pull up!)
On the battlefield	(Oh, yes)	(Hallelujah!)
You	(You)	(Well)
Can easy	(Oh, Lord)	(Now)
Be	(Yes, sir!)	(Well)
Tied	(Oh, yes!)	(Well)
As the Devil	(Yes, sir)	(Now)
On Earth	(Oh, yes!)	(Oh, yes!)
Hitler	(Oh, yes)	(Well)

And Hell	(Oh, yes!)	(And Hell!)
You	(You!)	(You!)
That speak	(Oh, yeah)	(Well)
The policies	(Oh, Lord)	(Policies)
For your country	(Oh, Lord)	(Well)
Hitler	(Yes, sir)	(Well)
And Hell	(Yes, sir!)	(And Hell!)
You	(Oh, yes)	(Well)
Say, "Go!" —	(Yes!)	(Glory!)
Men must go;	(Yes, sir!)	(Pull up there!)
Say, "Come" —	(Yes, sir)	(Well)
Then they must come	(Oh, Lord)	(Hallelujah!)
You,	(Yes, sir!)	(You!)
If you order them,	(Oh yes, sir)	(Well)
Their	(Oh, yes)	(Yes)
Necks	(Yes, sir)	(Yes)
Separate	(Oh, Lord)	(Yes)
From their bodies,	(Oh, Lord)	(Help me, Lord!)
It must be done	(Yes)	(Amen!)
Hitler,	(Oh, yes)	(Well)
You must come down!	(Oh yes, you must)	(Must come down!)
You, you too high	(Oh, yes)	(Well)
There's only one God	(Oh, yes)	(Well)
And you must come down!	(Yes, sir!)	(Hallelujah!)
I'm thinkin now	(Oh, Lord)	(Well)
Of innocent	(Oh, Lord)	(Innocent)
Children	(Oh, Lord)	(Yes)
And womens dyin	(Yes, sir)	(Yes)
All over	(Yes!)	(Pull up there!)
The land and country	(Yes, sir)	(Hallelujah!)

As	(Yes, sir)	(Well)
You come crushin through	(Oh, yes)	(Now)
Like the Demon of Hell	(Yes, sir)	(Yes)
On Earth	(Oh, yeah!)	(Well)
Hitler,	(Oh, yes)	(Well)
You must come down!	(Yes, you must!)	(Pull up there!)
Soon,	(Oh, yeah)	(Glory!)
Sooner or late	(Oh, yeah)	(Hallelujah!)
You must pay the price	(Yes, sir!)	(Well)
At the judgement bar	(Oh, Lord)	(Hallelujah!)

(Sung in harmony by all three voices)

Hitler, God's got his eyes on you
Hitler, God's got his eyes on you
Well, he sees all you do (Lord)
And he hears every word you say
Hitler, God's got his eyes on you

You is a stand-in	(Yes, sir!)	(Well)
Lib'ary	(Oh, yes)	(Pull up!)
For your peoples in Germany	(Oh, yeah)	(Oh, you is)
You	(Yes, sir!)	(Well)
Is a walkin	(Oh, yeah!)	(Hallelujah!)
And talkin	(Oh, Lord)	(Hallelujah!)
Inside torpedoes	(Sir)	(Pull up there!)
For your peoples in Germany	(Yes!)	(Yeah)
You	(Oh, yeah!)	(Yes!)
Must come down!	(Oh, yes!)	(Must come down!) :

For a more conditional sermon curse, one which offers the opportunity for repentance, see *Will You Spend Your Eternity in Hell?* by "Black Billy Sunday" — Reverend Dr. J. Gordon McPherson — at:
  LuckyMojo.com/will-you-spend-your-eternity-in-hell.html

Bible Spells Old and New

STEADY WORK, MONEY, SUCCESS, GAMBLING

HELP WITH A JOB INTERVIEW

Blend Steady Work and Crown of Success oils and anoint a square piece of paper with a five spot and write one of these verses on the paper:

Psalms 90:17: *"And let the beauty of the Lord our God be upon us: and establish thou the work of our hands upon us; yea, the work of our hands establish thou it."*

Luke 11:9: *"And I say unto you, Ask, and it shall be given you; seek, and ye shall find; knock, and it shall be opened unto you."*

Write over the verse your own words, such as, "May the job I seek at [Company] be mine!" Fold the paper towards yourself, turn it clockwise, and fold it again. Wear it in your left shoe when you go to the job interview.

MS. MELANIE'S THREE DAY MONEY MIRACLE SPELL

Dress three green candles with Money Drawing Oil from top to bottom. Grind together Irish Moss, Alfalfa, and Bayberry root chips. Add in sifted Pyrite Grit and Magnetic Sand. Roll the dressed candles in the mix. (If you prefer, you may prepare these as wax-rolled candles by adding the oil, herbs, and minerals to the melted wax.) Burn one candle per day for three days while praying the Three Day Miracle Prayer:

"Holy Trinity, who gives me insight on how to attain my goals and visions and the gift to forgive all those who have trespassed against me, including all those who are involved in my life. I want to thank you for all my blessings and to confirm with you once more that my faith is never wavering and I shall not be separated from you again no matter how many worldly desires I may encounter. I want to be with you and my loved ones, basking in your glory. Amen!" Then state your request.

MAMA MICKI'S PRAYER FOR SLOT MACHINE PLAYERS

For those who like to play slots pray Job 20:18 over your money, tokens, or machine before playing it:

"He hath swallowed down riches, and he shall vomit them up again: God shall cast them out of his belly."

JABEZ PRAYER TO CHANGE JOBS OR GET PROMOTED
To move around in your company by either promotion or relocation, first dress a candle with Boss Fix and Influence Oil. Then while you burn the candle pray over it the famous Jabez Prayer from 1 Chronicles 4:10:
"And Jabez called on the God of Israel, saying, Oh that thou wouldest bless me indeed, and enlarge my coast, and that thine hand might be with me, and that thou wouldest keep me from evil, that it may not grieve me! And God granted him that which he requested."

IF YOU HAVE DONE A JOB AND NOT BEEN PAID
If you have performed work and not yet received payment for your labours, write any — or all — of the following portions of Scripture on a petition paper in pencil. Over the text write the name of the person who owes you money, just one time, in ink. Cross the person's name with your own name, also written once in ink, to form a cross. Dress the four corners and the center of the paper with Pay Me Now Oil or Sachet Powder.
- **Leviticus 19:13:** *"The wages of him that is hired shall not abide with thee all night until the morning."*
- **Deuteronomy 24:15:** *"At his day thou shalt give him his hire, neither shall the sun go down upon it; for he is poor, and setteth his heart upon it: lest he cry against thee unto the LORD, and it be sin unto thee."*
- **Deuteronomy 25:4:** *"Thou shalt not muzzle the ox when he treadeth out the corn."*
- **Proverbs 3:28:** *"Say not unto thy neighbour, Go, and come again, and to morrow I will give; when thou hast it by thee."*
- **Romans 13:4:** *"Render therefore to all their dues: tribute to whom tribute is due."*
- **1 Corinthians 9:9:** *"For it is written in the law of Moses, Thou shalt not muzzle the mouth of the ox that treadeth out the corn."*
- **1 Timothy 5:18:** *"For the scripture saith, Thou shalt not muzzle the ox that treadeth out the corn. And, The labourer is worthy of his reward."*
- **James 5:4:** *"Behold, the hire of the labourers who have reaped down your fields, which is of you kept back by fraud, crieth: and the cries of them which have reaped are entered into the ears of the Lord of sabaoth."*

You may place the prepared paper under a Pay Me Vigil Candle, carry it in your wallet or mojo bag, or, if you have the courage and the situation warrants strong action, nail it to the person's door.

LUCKY MONEY BESAMIM SPICES

Besamim is a traditional spice mixture used every week by Jews at the Havdalah, a brief ceremony marking the formal conclusion to the Sabbath on Saturday nights. Specific ingredients and their number vary from maker to maker, but besamim is required to be fragrant, for its aroma is inhaled while praying thankfully to God for the creation of the "varieties of spices."

In hoodoo, besamim has long been marketed as a Lucky Money Herb Mix and many people report that it is a powerful tool for drawing wealth. Mix together Cinnamon, Cloves, Myrtle, Hyssop, Rosemary, Anise, and Bay Leaf. You may inhale the scent, burn the mixture as incense, add it to a bath, dress money with it, or use it to roll candles in, while praying: *"Lord God who made the sweet perfumes, sweeten my money matters."*

THE "FALL IN LOVE WITH LEARNING" PSALMS 134 SPELL

If you are struggling in school, this spell will help you banish discouragement and graduate with honours, enabling you to succeed in your chosen career. It is designed to transform those oppressive, dull texts, and assignments into attractive ideas that draw your attention!

Start by taking a bath using the Cast Off Evil Bath Crystals to remove negativity. During the bath recite or read aloud Psalms 136, because as it says in every verse of this Psalm, God's *"mercy endureth for ever."*

Follow the Cast Off Evil bath with a bath of King Solomon Wisdom and Attraction Bath Crystals mixed together. Save a little of the bathwater to add to your laundry rinse, grooming supplies, and cleaning supplies. Wash your floors with it too and sprinkle some on the floor of the car, so you'll put your feet in it and track it all over school.

Then, write Psalms 134 on a small piece of paper dressed with both King Solomon Wisdom Oil and Crown of Success Oil:

"Behold, bless ye the Lord, all ye servants of the Lord, which by night stand in the house of the Lord. Lift up your hands in the sanctuary, and bless the Lord. The Lord that made heaven and earth bless thee out of Zion."

Wrap the prayer paper around a small John the Conqueror Root and keep it in a mojo bag in your bra, pinned to your briefs, or on a string around your neck. Dust your schoolbooks and writing paper with King Solomon Wisdom and Attraction Sachet Powder. Anoint your laptop, glasses, pens and pencils with Attraction Oil. It's time to fall in love with learning and make school fall in love with you.

PROF. PORTERFIELD'S LUCKY NUMBER FIND SPELL
Write the numbers 1 through 9 on a white sheet of paper, first in red ink and then again on the back of the sheet of paper in green ink, running backwards, 9 through 1. Cut the numbers apart until you have nine small squares, each with the same number on both sides, one green and one red.

This is your 'Flock' with which you will discover your lucky numbers. Pray Psalms 77 over the 'Flock' as you hold your right thumb over each of the numbers. Take a clear, clean jar or a flat glass flask with a lid and place half of a package of Lucky Number Sachet Powder and your 'Flock' numbers in it. Seal the jar and anoint its lid with Lucky Number Oil.

When you want lucky numbers, turn the jar or flask over three times, each time repeating, "Luck is in my favour. Grant me the luck of my desires. My soul is strong in the Lord. Show me the Numbers, and I can do no wrong." Gently shake the jar or flask, and the numbers facing up in green are the numbers you need for this day. The numbers facing up in red are numbers to be avoided.

This spell should not be done more than once a week.

SEVEN DAY STEADY WORK SPELL
Mark a green candle into seven parts. Place it on a flat stone, and anoint it with seven drops of Steady Work Oil as you read Proverbs 16:3 *("Commit thy works unto the Lord, and thy thoughts shall be established.")* over it. Write the jobs you desire on a clean piece of paper and place the paper under the rock along with a one dollar bill as you say the following: *"I have paid the price through my misfortunes. Grant me this job, I pray, O Lord."* Burn one part of the candle each day for a week until the candle is consumed.

SAVE MONEY IN YOUR BIBLE
Open your Bible to the 23rd Psalm. Place a $5.00, $10.00, or larger bill at Psalms 23 and recite the Psalm. Each week add another bill at the start of each book of the Bible until you run through the entire Bible and return back to Psalms 23. Alternatively, you may count seven pages, and place a bill at every 7th page, or count 23 pages between bills.

You may start spending when the Bible is filled or make a second pass through, replacing each bill with another of higher value. You may also start a second Bible, and a third. One woman we know who did this for years actually lost count of how much money she had — and how many Bibles!

RECOVERING PEOPLE AND GOODS

FATHER, SON AND HOLY GHOST RETURN STOLEN GOODS
A talented root worker of Memphis, Tennessee, tells us that if a person steals something valuable from you and you want the thief to return it, or if you wish to encourage estranged or missing people to return home, you should prepare a name paper as follows:

In the name of the Father, Son, and Holy Ghost
[the person's name]
In the name of the Father, Son, and Holy Ghost
[the person's name]
In the name of the Father, Son, and Holy Ghost
[the person's name]

While you pray for the Lord to bring back the thief or the missing person, turn the paper sideways and write the same thing again, on top of the first writing. Put it under a "saint lamp," that is, a votive or novena candle such as you might commonly see in a Catholic church. We're told that in three days' time whatever you pray for will come true.

A LAMP TO GUIDE HOME
A traditional worker from Mobile, Alabama, offers the following way to bring a person back home: Take a brand new lamp or candle and a clean sheet of white paper. Write the person's name or initials nine times on the paper; turn the paper clockwise and write your name over the previous writing three times. Roll the paper up, rolling it toward you, just as you want that person to come home to you. Then put the paper under the lamp and say: *"In the name of the Father, the Son and the Holy Ghost come home now where you belong."* Burn the lamp for nine days, and when they come home, pinch, don't blow, the lamp out.

FOR OBTAINING INFORMATION
To obtain information about a lost person, a mysterious person, or lost goods, inscribe the name of the person or thing you wish to gather information about, into the wax of a white candle, and anoint it with a combination of Clarity Oil and Compelling Oil. Pray Luke 8:17: *"For nothing is secret, that shall not be made manifest; neither any thing hid, that shall not be known and come abroad"* while burning the candle.

LOVE, FAMILY, AND RECONCILIATION

TO DISCOVER YOUR FUTURE MATE

To discover the identity of your future mate open a Bible and put a key in the Bible, traditionally a skeleton key is used for this, letting the head of the key protrude beyond the edge of the pages. Rest the tip of the finger on the key and say aloud Ruth 1:16:

"And Ruth said, Intreat me not to leave thee, or to return from following after thee: for whither thou goest, I will go; and where thou lodgest, I will lodge: thy people shall be my people, and thy God my God:"

Continue by repeating the alphabet; the letter upon which the key turns will be the initial of your future husband.

TO MAKE A "MAMA'S BOY" INTO A GREAT HUSBAND

If your husband listens to his mother more than you and is always comparing her against you, then here is a way to cleave him to you:

Obtain one red male Adam and one red female Eve figural candle, one for you and one for him. Dress them both in Adam and Eve Oil, place them so they face each other, and tie them together around their loins with red sewing thread. Light them and recite Genesis 2:24:

"Therefore shall a man leave his father and his mother and shall cleave unto his wife, and they will be one flesh."

HEALING LOVE BETWEEN A COUPLE USING PSALMS 45

Godfrey Selig tells us that Psalms 45 and 46 are said to possess the virtue of making peace between man and wife, especially to tame cross wives. If you have a scolding or nagging wife, pronounce the 45th Psalm *("My heart is inditing a good matter: I speak of the things which I have made touching the king: my tongue is the pen of a ready writer...")* over pure Olive oil, and anoint your body with it. This will make your wife be in a more loveable and friendly mood. However, if a man has innocently incurred the enmity of his wife and desires a proper return of conjugal love and peace, he should pray the 46th Psalm *("God is our refuge and strength, a very present help in trouble...")* over the Olive oil, then anoint his wife thoroughly with it, and married love will return. The two Psalms can be recited sequentially and a couple also can make these prayers together, anointing each other as thoroughly as they wish.

MISS CAT'S PINK CANDLES AND PSALMS 32
When one feels that a friendship or love break may have arisen in part due to one's own headstrong or "mulish" actions, dress pink candles with Reconciliation Oil and read Psalms 32 over them. As you read it, realize that verses 1 through 7 are as spoken by the petitioner, and verses 8 through 11 are as spoken by the Lord in reply. You will read the entire Psalm over the candles as they burn with that understanding.

PEACEFUL HOME FOR A TROUBLESOME HUSBAND
If you have a cantankerous, domineering, or argumentative husband and wish to have a peaceful home, here is a solid old time way to fix that mess and turn things in a better direction:

Pray Psalms 140 every day as you rise from your bed while you do the following five things, once each, in the order given, on as many days as it takes you. Don't worry if it takes several days or weeks:

- Place Poppy seeds in the four corners of each room in the house while reciting Mark 4:8; this is to lull his mind and gentle him.
- Every other day, fumigate the house with Peaceful Home Incense, reciting Psalms 44. (If you can't use incense, spritz with Peace Water.)
- Anoint a small cross with Peaceful Home Oil while reciting Psalms 136, and carry it on you at all times. If you can get your husband to carry one, then do so as well, but don't tell him what it's for.
- Secretly sprinkle Commanding Powder in your husband's right shoe as you say the following *"Now [his full name] I'm tired of all this argument. You be at peace, and know I love you, [his full name]."*
- Sprinkle Van Van Oil into warm scrub water and wipe down all of the the door frames and window frames of your house.

MARY BEE'S HONEYCOMB AND THE SONG OF SOLOMON
For an extra boost to a sugar or honey jar spell that is to be worked to sweeten a lover or mate, get a piece of honeycomb. Lay the honeycomb out on a cookie sheet and push it down until it's flat. On a clean piece of paper write out the portion of the Song of Solomon that best suits your piece of work and then write your personal petition on top of it. Fold up the petition and place it in the center of the honeycomb. Fold up the honeycomb around the petition, and push the honeycomb down into your sugar or honey jar. Light candles on top as you normally would.

TO ATTRACT A LOVER

Pray Psalms 89 three times daily for nine days after 6:30 a.m. As you do so, anoint yourself over your heart with Come To Me Oil.

On each of the nine days as you prepare yourself to meet a new special someone burn three teaspoons of Come To Me Incense and place some Attraction Oil on your neck or wrists.

On the fifth day of the work write out five different letters of the alphabet, representing possible names of new lovers, on five small slips of paper and dress them with either Follow Me Boy or Follow Me Girl Oil, depending on your desires. Place one slip in each shoe and the others in your clothing, look your best, and get ready for a new lover.

RECONCILING A TROUBLED MARRIAGE

To help a troubled marriage, get a light blue Bride and Groom Candle. Dress the candle toward you from head to foot with Reconciliation Oil, and then sprinkle it with Peaceful Home Sachet Powder.

Before lighting the candle, recite Hosea 2:18-20:

"And in that day will I make a covenant for them with the beasts of the field and with the fowls of heaven, and with the creeping things of the ground: and I will break the bow and the sword and the battle out of the earth, and will make them to lie down safely. And I will betroth thee unto me for ever; yea, I will betroth thee unto me in righteousness, and in judgment, and in lovingkindness, and in mercies. I will even betroth thee unto me in faithfulness: and thou shalt know the Lord."

Burn the candle all at once to the end. When the candle has burned out, say a heartfelt prayer to God thanking him for his gifts and again asking him to heal your marriage.

TO REKINDLE YOUR MAN'S PASSION

Inscribe a red Penis Candle with the name of the man to be worked on, and then dress it with Fire of Love Oil, handling it in an intimate way. As you prepare to light it, recite Proverbs 5:18-19: *"Let thy fountain be blessed: and rejoice with the wife of thy youth. Let her be as the loving hind and pleasant roe; let her breasts satisfy thee at all times; and be thou ravished always with her love."* For added 'oomph' also recite this same portion as you sprinkle Fire of Love Sachet Powder in your bed and in his underpants drawer.

FOR A SOON-TO-BE FAMILY OF THREE

For a couple expecting their first child, get a white Adam Candle and a white Eve Candle to represent you and your partner. Take a small ball of white wax and fix it to the Eve Candle's belly by dripping wax over it and forming it with your fingers until Eve looks pregnant. Name and bless the two figures, carving each of your names on your respective figure with a brand new needle with a golden eye.

Dress the candles toward you from head to toe with Blessing Oil, Healing Oil, Prosperity Oil, and herbs for motherhood and health such as Angelica powder, Flax seed, and Motherwort.

Place the candles side by side, draw a circle around them with Blessing Sachet Powder, and recite aloud John 15:12-17: *"This is my commandment, That ye love one another, as I have loved you. Greater love hath no man than this, that a man lay down his life for his friends. Ye are my friends, if ye do whatsoever I command you. Henceforth I call you not servants; for the servant knoweth not what his lord doeth: but I have called you friends; for all things that I have heard of my Father I have made known unto you. Ye have not chosen me, but I have chosen you, and ordained you, that ye should go and bring forth fruit, and that your fruit should remain: that whatsoever ye shall ask of the Father in my name, he may give it you. These things I command you, that ye love one another."*

Follow the verses with this prayer: *"Oh Lord, I call upon you, Father, Son, and Holy Ghost. Almighty Trinity, bless my trinity-to-be. Please Lord, I have done as you commanded, and I ask humbly that you bless my family and my home. Bless this pregnancy and let it be ideal. Keep us healthy, father and mother, and may our baby grow healthy and strong. If it's your will, may we prosper, and may our home know peace throughout this time of change and beyond. In the name of the Father, Son, and Holy Ghost I pray; Amen."*

Light the candles, and let them burn straight through.

TO GET A MAN TO KEEP YOU WELL

For a working girl, if you want a man to keep you in good circumstances, get a Follow Me Boy Vigil Candle. Dedicate the candle in the man's name, and recite Psalms 18:19: *"He brought me forth also into a large place; he delivered me, because he delighted in me."* Burn during the evening hours until it's done.

HELPING, BLESSING, AND HEALING

We do not present these healing spells as a substitute for any form of professional medical consultation, care, or treatment. They are simply traditional in our community and we hold them in high regard, believing as we do that the healing sought and conveyed by them comes from a higher spiritual power.

CONJUREMAN ALI 'S EASY CHILDBIRTH SPELL

For a safe childbirth bathe yourself with Blessing Bath Crystals while praying Psalms 33 (*"Rejoice in the Lord, O ye righteous: for praise is comely for the upright"*). Before labour use 7-11 Holy Oil to draw a cross on your stomach and another cross on your forehead, each time praying Psalms 33. This will help ease childbirth and ensure the safety of you and your child.

PETITIONING SAINT LAZARUS FOR SKIN RASHES

Saint Lazarus the Beggar (Luke 16-31) is the patron saint of skin problems. If your dermatologist allows it, wash with a dilute solution of Saint Lazarus Bath Crystals in Holy Water while reciting Luke 17:11-19 and petitioning Saint Lazarus for intercession. Luke 17:11-19 recounts how Jesus cleansed the ten lepers. Be sure to offer thanks afterwards.

OLD GERMAN SPELL TO STOP BLEEDING WITH EZEKIEL

This old tradition to stop bleeding came to America with German immigrants. To accomplish the goal one recites over the wound Ezekiel 16:6: *"And when I passed by thee, and saw thee polluted in thine own blood, I said unto thee when thou wast in thy blood, Live; yea, I said unto thee when thou wast in thy blood, Live."*

ANOTHER BLOOD STOPPING SPELL

This is often called a certain remedy to stop bleeding, which is said to cure no matter how far away a person is, so long as their first name is rightly pronounced while using it. Call upon the Lord by saying aloud:
"Jesus Christ dearest blood!
That stoppeth the pain and stoppeth the blood,
In this help you [the person in need's first name only],
God the Father, God the Son, God the Holy Ghost. Amen."

BACKACHE MASSAGE CURE WITH PSALMS 3
If you suffer from severe backaches, write out a copy of Psalms 3 onto a clean sheet of paper and then burn it to ashes. Mix the ashes with Olive Oil or 7-11 Holy Oil and a few drops of Peppermint Oil. Pray Psalms 3 over the mixture as well, then use the mixture to massage your back.

A BIBLE SPELL FOR PROBLEMS GETTING PREGNANT
To help with problems in conceiving a child while under a doctor's care, you'll need to get the medical staff to assist you. Obtain Bay leaves, Squaw Vine, Master Root, Angelica Root, Queen Elizabeth Root chips, Healing Bath Crystals, Influence Oil and Sachet Powders, and Dr. Jose Gregorio Hernandez Oil, Bath Crystals, and Sachet Powders.

On a Monday, begin by laying Bay leaves around your working space; they bring favour and keep people from noticing anything they don't need to see. Make a bath-tea by simmering the herbs and roots for ten minutes. Strain the tea and scatter the herbs and roots in your yard. Dissolve the bath crystals in the liquid. This strong bath-tea will keep for three days in the fridge or you may freeze it into ice cubes and thaw them as needed.

Dilute your bath-tea with warm water if it is too strong. Wash yourself upward, paying special attention to your belly. Mark your belly with a cross and pray Psalms 128, except that where in verse 3 it says, *"Thy wife shall be as a fruitful vine..."* say instead, *"I shall be as a fruitful vine..."*

Dress all your insurance and medical papers with Influence and Dr. Jose Gregorio Hernandez powders. Dress your phone with Dr. Jose Gregorio Hernandez and Influence oils. Whenever you go see the doctor or an insurance person face to face, dress the soles of your shoes so you track the oils into their office, and they and their staff will track it everywhere.

FRUITS OF THE SPIRIT ARTHRITIS SPELL
To help with arthritis, take a box of golden raisins and place them in a shallow lidded container. Cover the raisins with gin as you recite aloud Galatians 5:22-23: *"But the fruit of the Spirit is love, joy, peace, longsuffering, gentleness, goodness, faith, meekness, temperance: against such there is no law."* Put the lid on the container and let the raisins soak for two to three weeks. Each day take nine raisins from the jar, recite Jeremiah 17:14: *"Heal me, O Lord, and I shall be healed; save me, and I shall be saved: for thou art my praise"* over them, and eat them.

SKULL CANDLE FOR MENTAL HEALING

Take a small square of white paper and write out on it Deuteronomy 31:8: *"And the Lord, he it is that doth go before thee; he will be with thee, he will not fail thee, neither forsake thee: fear not, neither be dismayed."*

Turn the paper clockwise and write your name seven times over the Bible verse. Dress the paper by making a five spot pattern of small crosses on it with Cast Off Evil Oil. Then place a few White or Yellow Mustard seeds, a pinch of Five Finger Grass, and a crumb of Dragon's Blood resin in the paper. Fold it toward you, then turn it and fold it again. With a knife or other sharp object, carve a hole in the bottom of a white Skull Candle large enough to hold the folded paper packet. Melt the left-over wax in a spoon and use it to seal the hole back up. Burn the candle in sections for at least half an hour a day while reciting Deuteronomy 31:8 and Psalms 23. A Skull Candle burned in this way will last for weeks.

A SIMPLE PRAYER FOR THE HOMELESS

Take a few dollar bills and dress them with a lucky oil such as Blessing, Van Van, Fast Luck, or even Black Cat by making small crosses on them in a five spot pattern while praying Psalms 145:16 as you do so: *"Thou openest thine hand, and satisfiest the desire of every living thing."*

Place the bills in your wallet in such a way that you can distinguish them from your "regular" money. When a homeless person asks you for change, ask them their name. Say, *"Lord, open your hand and satisfy every righteous desire of my brother/sister [name]."* Give them the bill, explaining that it has been dressed for their good luck.

AURA LAFOREST'S COIN WASH

Collect a double handful of shiny, brand-new coins in assorted denominations. Prepare a bath-tea with equal parts whole Cloves, Allspice berries, and Blue Flag root, plus a drop of honey. Strain the tea into a wash basin and "wash" each coin between your hands as you pray Psalms 23. Let the coins dry on a clean white cloth. When you go out in the streets, distribute the coins to the poor, for as it says in Deuteronomy 15:7: *"If there be among you a poor man of one of thy brethren within any of thy gates in thy land which the Lord thy God giveth thee, thou shalt not harden thine heart, nor shut thine hand from thy poor brother:"* For this good deed you will be blessed.

SELF-BLESSING AND SELF-FORGIVENESS RITUAL BATH

For this ritual you will need Hyssop, salt, two small white candles, Blessing Oil, a photo of yourself, and a Bible.

Start just before sunrise. Set the two white candles on either side of your tub so you pass between them as you enter the bath. Draw the bath and add Hyssop to the water, either in the form of herb-tea or prepared supplies such as Hyssop Bath Crystals or Hyssop Oil. Light the candles and recite the 23rd Psalm as you enter the bath. Soak in the water, and when ready, pour water over your head while reciting Psalms 51:7: *"Purge me with Hyssop, and I shall be clean: wash me, and I shall be whiter than snow."* When you feel ready, stand up and step backwards out of the tub between the two candles and say, *"In Jesus name, Amen."*

Save a cupful of the bathwater before draining the tub. Take this water to a crossroads, and throw it backwards over your shoulder, to the East. Walk away without looking back.

TO AID A MAN'S NATURE

A man may use this to aid his nature if he has not been tied down or jinxed. Obtain John the Conqueror Bath Crystals, a John the Conqueror Root, Nature Oil, a white Penis Candle, and small muslin cloth bag.

On a Saturday morning bathe with John the Conqueror Bath Crystals, reciting aloud Judges 16:28: *"And Samson called unto the Lord, and said, O Lord God, remember me, I pray thee, and strengthen me, I pray thee, only this once, O God."* After the bath take the John the Conquer Root and the white Penis Candle and anoint them both with Nature Oil, always anointing them with movements towards you as you recite aloud from the Song of Solomon 7:7: *"Your stature is like a palm tree…."*

Put the John the Conqueror Root into the muslin bag, pin it to your underwear, and wear it for three days. Burn the candle as the hands of the clock are rising in three sections over three days. After that you may carry the root in your pocket or keep it between the box springs and mattress of your bed.

MORNING RITE FOR SELF-BLESSING

Recite Psalms 34:8 over a glass of spring water or seltzer: *"O taste and see that the Lord is good: blessed is the man that trusteth in him."* Then drink the water and set about your day's activities.

AFFIRMATION OF PRAYER REQUEST WITH PSALMS 66
Write a prayer on one side of a narrow slip of paper, and on the other side, Psalms 66:19: *"Verily God hath heard me; he hath attended to the voice of my prayer."* Wrap the slip around the base of an offertory candle, Psalm side outward, glue the end down, and burn the candle in a pan of clean sand.

WALLS OF JERICHO ROAD OPENER SPELL
Before dawn while the hands of the clock are rising dissolve half a packet of Road Opener Bath Crystals into a tub of hot water. Pour the water over your head nine times as you recite Joshua 6:12: *"And Joshua rose early in the morning, and the priests took up the ark of the Lord"* This is in remembrance of the day Joshua brought down the walls of Jericho and opened the way before them into the city.

After the bath let yourself to air-dry and collect a cup, bowl, or basin of the used bath water, which now has your essence in it. Dress in fresh, clean clothes (particularly your socks and underwear) that have been lightly dusted with Road Opener Sachet Powder, saying, *"Let the road be opened before me as the walls of Jericho were made open before Joshua"* as you do so.

Carry the remnant bath-water to a crossroads and throw the water toward the sunrise in the East, saying Joshua 20: *"So the people shouted when the priests blew with the trumpets: and it came to pass, when the people heard the sound of the trumpet, and the people shouted with a great shout, that the wall fell down flat, so that the people went up into the city, every man straight before him, and they took the city."* Walk home and don't look back!

When you return home, take an orange offertory candle and carve your full name on it with a brand new, unused needle and dress it with Road Opener Oil. As you dress it, speak aloud Psalms 107:13-16:

"Then they cried unto the Lord in their trouble, and he saved them out of their distresses. He brought them out of darkness and the shadow of death, and brake their bands in sunder. Oh that men would praise the Lord for his goodness, and for his wonderful works to the children of men! For he hath broken the gates of brass, and cut the bars of iron in sunder."

Burn the candle through to the end, no matter how long it takes.

Later dissolve the remaining half of the Road Opener Bath Crystals in hot water and add that to the rinse water of your laundry, especially your underwear and socks. When you wear these fixed clothes, you will be dressed for luck and ready to walk your newly opened road.

HARMING AND CURSING

CAROLINA DEAN'S PSALMS 109 CURSE OF A CO-WORKER
To curse a lazy, disrespectful workmate, first write the person's name nine times on a square paper. Turn the paper and write the words, "Back Down!" crossing and covering the person's name. Anoint the corners and center in a five spot with vinegar to "sour her life" until she does what you ask. Fold the paper away from yourself three times and set it aside.

Carve the person's name on a black candle, reversing the letters so that they appear as you would see them in a mirror. Turn the candle top for bottom, dress it with vinegar, and let it dry. Place the name paper under an upside-down saucer and set the reversed candle in a holder atop the saucer.

Light the candle and read Psalms 109 as the candle burns. If your target is female, then change the pronouns to match. For example, Psalms 109:7 reads, *"When he shall be judged, let him be condemned: and let his prayer become sin."* If your target is female you would change "he" to "she." As you read the Psalm, visualize the events mentioned therein happening to your enemy. After the candle is spent, take the name paper and press it in the Bible at Psalms 109 so that the words of the Psalm "press into" this person, and the vinegar will sour their life until they do what you ask.

TO FORCE SOMEONE TO DO AS YOU SAY
From a worker out of Savannah, Georgia, we hear that to force someone to do as you say, take a pencil and write your target's name on a plain piece of brown paper. Take that paper and fold it towards you as you say, *"In the Name of the Lord, Name of the Father, Son and Holy Ghost."* Next, put the paper under the insole of your shoe and wear it like that. Continue to wear the paper every day and you will just be able to conquer them any way that you want to.

CONJUREMAN ALI'S ENEMY SPELL WITH HOLY OIL
Carve your target's name on a purple candle along with your command, using a brand new gold eye needle. Anoint the candle with Holy Oil and burn it on top of a picture of the target or name paper while praying Psalms 114 *("When Israel went out of Egypt...")* and then Psalms 110 *("The Lord said unto my Lord, Sit thou at my right hand, until I make thine enemies thy footstool.")* in that order, and then call out your command as you do so.

MISS CAT'S CURSE ON AN EX BY KILLING HIS HONEY JAR

If you have made a honey jar and burned candles on it for a lover and now you hate him, you can kill the jar and curse him at the same time.

Carefully break the built-up candle wax off the jar, melt it down, make a waxen dollie of it, and baptize it in his name. If you had any personal concerns of his, include them in the doll. Get a bottle of Damnation Oil and a packet of pins. Heat each pin in fire until it is red-hot, then dip it in the Damnation Oil and stick it into the doll, starting with the eyes (so he cannot see what you are doing), proceeding through the traditional 13 points of pain, ending with his genitals, and cursing him all the while.

Lay the doll-baby on a cookie sheet which you can dispose of and will not miss. Cover him over and make a solid ring around him of Crossing Incense Powder, to mess him up in every way imaginable.

Open up the jar and pour out the contents around the ring of Crossing Incense Powder, in a second ring that does not touch the doll. Sweetness and love are forever to be out of his reach, and the ring of Crossing Incense Powder prevents him ever achieving happiness.

Lay down a ring of Jinx Incense Powder over-top the ring of sugar or honey to jinx any sweetness that even tried to approach him. Also cover over the doll-baby with Jinx Incense Powder.

Take this mess, on the cookie sheet, to a graveyard or to his front porch (!) and carefully lay it down. Sprinkle lighter fluid all around the ring of Jinx Incense Powder and spiral it inward through the ring of Crossing Incense Powder, and at last arrive, by continue to spiral it in, to the genitals of the doll-baby.

Strike a match and set the lighter fluid on fire. If you made this work well, the heat of the flaming and burning incense powder will melt the wax dollie and it will catch afire and be consumed utterly as you recite the following two Bible verses, with great emotion and depth of feeling:

"The Lord shall send upon thee cursing, vexation, and rebuke, in all that thou settest thine hand unto for to do, until thou be destroyed, and until thou perish quickly; because of the wickedness of thy doings, whereby thou hast forsaken me." (Deuteronomy 28:20). *For, behold, the Lord will come with fire, and with his chariots like a whirlwind, to render his anger with fury, and his rebuke with flames of fire."* (Isaiah 66:15).

This is a strong ritual conclusion to a spell which started one way (for sweetness) and ended another way (in anger).

CAUSE CONFUSION TO THOSE WHO MEAN YOU HARM

Get a photograph of your enemy, or something they have touched. This could be a cigarette butt, button, or the like, even a piece of mail. Place the article in a jar with a lid. Anoint the lid with three drops of Confusion Oil. Write out Psalms 2 *("Why do the heathen rage, and the people imagine a vain thing?")* on a sheet of paper and cut it into nine pieces. Burn Confusion Incense along with one segment of the prayer paper for nine days and add the ash to the jar each day. On the tenth day burn John the Conqueror Incense and sprinkle the ash from it towards where the one who means you harm lives. Bury the jar upside down in a graveyard while praying Psalms 2 aloud.

MAKING SOMEONE LEAVE: THE NINE SWITCHES SPELL

A conjure practitioner from Fayetteville, North Carolina relayed this unusual method of making someone leave town. First you cut a switch from each of nine different kinds of trees. Next take the nine switches to a body of running water. One by one throw the switches into the running water. Each time you throw a switch call the person's name and say, *"I hope to God so-and-so will leave; In the Name of the Father and the Holy Ghost."* Make sure to say their name and the prayer in a tone that indicates how badly you want them to leave. Do this for all nine switches, and soon your target will leave town.

TO RUN SOMEONE OUT OF TOWN

To drive off a bad neighbour or enemy, get a black D.U.M.E. (Death Unto My Enemies) Vigil Light and a plain white candle. Dress the D.U.M.E. candle with Red Pepper, Black Pepper, and Crossing Oil, and mark the glass in seven sections. Write the person's name on the back label.

Light the white candle first, as the hands of the clock are rising, and then light the D.U.M.E. Candle as the hands of the clock are falling. As the candles burn, recite Psalms 118 *("The Lord is on my side; I will not fear: what can man do unto me?")*. Repeat your enemy's name over the candles once a day. Each time the black candle burns to a line, write your enemy's name, tear it up, and scatter the name paper at the edge of town.

Once they move, write their name on brown paper, fold the paper away from you, put it into a bottle of Four Thieves Vinegar, and bury it in the graveyard. Recite Psalms 118 over the burial spot, and walk away.

THREE CURSES FROM HENRI GAMACHE

Henri Gamache's *The Master Book of Candle Burning*, written in 1942, remains the most influential text on candle magic in the conjure tradition. Less well known is Gamache's 1945 survey of world magic, *The Master Key to Occult Secrets*. The spells in these books range from benevolent healings to hateful curses. Many feature altar candles in symbolic colours, dressed with named condition oils. Quite a few also include the reading of Psalms from a Bible kept open upon the altar. Here are three spells against enemies.

TO AROUSE DISCORD, ANGER, OR JEALOUSY IN ANOTHER

Place two black Crucifix Candles dressed with Double Cross Oil at the left rear and right rear corners of your altar. In the center place an Astral Candle of the person who is the object of your wrath, dressed with Zodiac Oil. To the left of center, place a brown candle dressed with Domination Oil. To the right of center, place a black candle dressed with Inflammatory Confusion Oil. At the left front of the altar, place a Bible open to Psalms 70 and pray this Psalm as you burn the candles 15 minutes daily on Mondays and Fridays, for three weeks.

HOW TO CUT OFF AN ENEMY

If you have an enemy, get a little piece of their clothing and wrap or sew it up into a small packet, saying over it Psalms 143:12 *("Cut off mine enemies, and destroy all them that afflict my soul")* as you do so. Carry the packet on you or sew it into the lining of your coat or clothes. So long as you carry this, your enemy will be cut off from you and powerless to harm you.

TO CAUSE CONFUSION IN AN ENEMY

Place two white Crucifix Candles dressed with 7-11 Holy Oil at the left rear and right rear corners of your altar. On the center left side of the altar place an Astral Candle dedicated to your enemy and dressed with Zodiac Oil. On the right center side of the altar place a black candle dressed with Confusion Oil, and immediately to its left place an orange candle, which is also dressed with Confusion Oil. The black candle and the orange candle should be touching. At the left front of the altar, place a Bible open to Psalms 70 and pray this Psalm as you burn the candles 30 minutes daily each evening before retiring. The black candle only should be extinguished after the first reading of Psalms 70 each night..

PROTECTION AND JINX BREAKING

GETTING JUSTICE WITH THE TWELVE APOSTLES
The famous Laughing Doctor of Waycross, Georgia passed on this spell for getting justice. If someone has done something to you — killed some of your family, killed your livestock, or run somebody away from you that's kin to you — get a brand-new metal pie pan that never has been used. Inscribe the Lord's Prayer and the Twelve Disciples' names on it, and your name under that. Turn the pie pan over and inscribe what you want done to the person on the bottom of it. Then you bury the pie pan, bottom side up, under your doorstep, and whatever you wished and planned on this pie pan and wrote on it to be done, the Twelve Apostles, the Disciples, will get busy and do it. That will have to happen in 24 hours.

TO GET A COURT CASE DISMISSED
An old time court case work is to write the names of all Twelve Apostles on a Sage, Bay, or Plantain leaf. Place this in your right shoe. Write the name of the judge on paper, and place this in your left shoe. Your appearance will be delayed, and the third time you go, your case will be dismissed.

TO GET A JOB IN HARD TIMES
We hear out of Fayetteville, North Carolina, that if you wish to get a job, write the Twelve Apostles' names first in a column, and then write the boss's name 12 times in another column. Fold the paper and place it in the bottom of your shoe. Wear it for three days before your interview.

TO CALM AN ENEMY
From Brunswick, Georgia, comes this simple method to break a jinx by calming down an enemy and soothing the tensions that led the person who threw for you in the first place. Write out the names of the Apostles and below them write out Matthew 5:44: *"But I say to you, Love your enemies and pray for those who persecute you."* Below that write the name of the person that's angry with you. Fold up the prayer paper and put it in your shoe while saying Psalms 34:14 *"Depart from evil, and do good; seek peace, and pursue it."* Then wear it in your shoe. This will conquer them under the teachings and peace of Jesus Christ and keep them down easy.

AGAINST GHOSTS, SPIRITS, HAINTS, AND HAGS

- Ida James of Fort Valley, Georgia has passed down that when one is confronted by a ghost or troublesome spirit one should ask them directly, "What in the name of the Lord do you want?" They will then go away and leave you be or they will carry you to a place and tell you to dig until you find hidden monies.
- Allene Dicks of Natchez, Mississippi says if your house is being troubled by haints you should read a verse from the Bible backwards (Pick it at random or select from among your favourites.) Fold that page in half, place a knife and a fork within the fold, and put the Bible under your pillow. No haint can enter your house.
- Clara Luckett of Calhoun, Alabama advises that to keep a hag from riding you at night, you should place an open Bible beneath your pillow at night. The hag is compelled to count every letter in the Bible before she can be about the business of her nightly ride.
- Rena Franks of Columbus, Mississippi taught something similar. She said that to place a Bible with a cross mark made upon it under your pillow will keep hags from riding you.

UNJINXING A WHOLE FAMILY

To remove a jinx affecting the whole household, burn Jinx Killer Incense daily for each person hurt. Anoint them with Jinx Killer Oil, and read Psalms 9 *("I will praise thee, O Lord, with my whole heart")*. Do this daily for seven days. Sprinkle Jinx Killer Sachet Powder all around your yard. Wipe down your door, window frames, and uncarpeted floors with Cast Off Evil Oil. On carpeted areas, sprinkle with Cast Off Evil Sachet Powder and vacuum it up. Also for the entire seven days, all the baths taken in the house should have Jinx Killer Bath Crystals added to the bath water.

KEEP THE LAW AWAY WITH THE THREE HIGHEST NAMES

If the police are bothering you, get a brand new pack of gold eye needles and place one outside each corner of your house by burying it in a small hole with its head facing up so that the "eye" of the needle can look out for you. As you fill in each of the holes around the buried needles, say the following prayer: *"In the name of the Father, the Son, and the Holy Ghost. I pray God that the policeman stays away. In the name of the Father, the Son, and the Holy Ghost."*

TO STOP EVIL WITH PSALMS 60 AND THE LORD'S PRAYER
If you suspect someone is evil and causing harm, make a cross on the outer doors of your house with Holy Water. Make a cross over your heart with Run Devil Run Oil. Read Psalms 60 at dawn and sunset.

Write the name of the person you suspect on parchment paper in black ink. If you are unsure who the evil is coming from then write "all my enemies." Draw a cross in each corner of the paper. Place the paper in a jar with Cast Off Evil Sachet Powder.

Burn a white candle dressed with Cast Off Evil Oil and drop three drops of wax on the parchment paper every day for five days. While the white candle is burning, burn Cast Off Evil Incense. Also recite the Lord's Prayer while the candle is burning.

On the sixth day take the jar to running water and sprinkle the sachet powder and the parchment paper into the running water. Do not watch the water run as you pour or afterwards. It is said that to recapture its strength the evil will follow the water.

When you go home, wash your floors with Cast Off Evil floor wash, and then bathe with Power Bath Crystals to add to your spiritual power.

REVERSING A CROSSED CONDITION
If you find yourself crossed and you want to send it back to the one who crossed you, first use black ink to write their name backward, as if you were seeing it reflected in a mirror, onto a piece of parchment paper no bigger than the palm of your right hand. Turn it over and write your impression of the crossing on the other side of the paper, again in black ink. Burn Reversing Incense daily for nine days. Anoint the parchment paper with Reversing Oil, and pass it through the smoke each day. Put the ashes from the incense into a jar with a lid. Anoint the lid of the jar with Protection Oil. Seal the jar with red wax.

On the ninth day after passing the parchment paper through the smoke, burn it and put the ashes in an envelope addressed to the one you are reversing the crossing onto. Seal the envelope with red wax. Use a sticker stamp or moisten the stamp with water only. Do not lick the stamp or the envelope. Read Psalms 1. Be sure to anoint the heels of your feet with Reversing Oil for nine more days and also bathe with Reversing Bath Crystals. Take the letter and the jar and dispose of them at the crossroads, then walk away and do not look back.

THE EVIL EYE

The evil eye is a kind of sickness, jinx, or curse that is put on someone, usually without intention, by an envious, jealous, or covetous person. While not universal, belief in the evil eye is widely found around the world and it is mentioned in the Bible. In Hebrew it is called ayin ha-ra (the evil eye). In Italian it is malocchio (the bad eye), in Sicilian it is jettatura (projection [from the eye]), in Spanish mal ojo or el ojo (the bad eye or the eye). In Sweden it is onda ögat (an evil look) and in Turkey nazar (the eye).

It is believed that a person who is not particularly evil or wicked can harm you, your children, your livestock, or your fruit trees, by simply looking at them with envy, jealousy, or covetousness and praising them. This is not necessarily done with a wicked intention. The effect of the evil eye is misfortune, but the person who harbours the jealousy or covetousness and gives the evil eye is not necessarily an evil person.

THE HAND OF MIRIAM AGAINST THE EVIL EYE

Obtain a hamsa hand, also known a hand of Miriam amulet, and anoint it with Cast Off Evil Oil while saying Psalms 23. When this is done the charm should be placed in the front doorway of the house, in a front window facing out, over a child's crib or stroller, or, if of safe size, given as a charm for the child or adult to wear.

BREAK THE EVIL EYE WITH AN EGG CLEANSING

If you believe you have come under the influence of the evil eye, take a fresh egg and move it over your body in downward strokes from the top of your head down to the bottoms of your feet while praying aloud from Deuteronomy 15:9: *"Beware that there be not a thought in thy wicked heart, saying, The seventh year, the year of release, is at hand; and thine eye be evil against thy poor brother, and thou givest him nought; and he cry unto the Lord against thee, and it be sin unto thee."* Follow that by reciting Psalms 23.

Then take the egg and break it into a clean saucer and place the saucer under the affected person's bed, or if this cannot be done, place the saucer by the left hand bed side. Make sure that this egg will not be ingested or meddled with by pets or small children.

After an evening and a day have passed, take the saucer to the crossroads, toss it over your left shoulder into the crossroads, immediately walk away, and do not look back.

At the End

FREQUENTLY ASKED QUESTIONS

The Lucky Mojo Forum was started in 2008. Averaging sixty posts per day, it is an online community in which questions are answered daily with regards to the practice of hoodoo and the use of Lucky Mojo spiritual supplies. The Forum is open to all, and anyone can join and ask questions. The Lucky Mojo Forum can be accessed online at:
Forum.LuckyMojo.com

Answers to questions, be they in the form of advice, encouragement, clarification, or spell suggestions, are provided by both forum members and a dedicated team of moderators who are all graduates of catherine yronwode's Hoodoo Rootwork Correspondence Course.

Read more about the Hoodoo Rootwork Correspondence Course at:
LuckyMojo.com/mojocourse.html

The Frequently Asked Questions and the answers that follow have been selected from the voluminous body of information on the Forum regarding traditional hoodoo practices and are intended to complete and augment the information that is included in the preceding pages. Here you will find answers to some of the most commonly asked questions in the Forum regarding the intersection between religion and magic.

When reading the answers to the questions provided, note that usernames followed by an (M) are people who are or were at one time Forum moderators. Those marked (M, AIRR) are moderators who are also in professional practice as members of the Association of Independent Readers and Rootworkers:

catherine yronwode	ConjureMan Ali
Mary Bee	Lukianos
Miss Michaele	Deacon Millett
Professor Ames	Miss Bri
Leah Rivera	Professor Porterfield

These AIRR members can be reached for personal readings, magical coaching, candle services, and custom spell-casting at the AIRR web site:
ReadersAndRootworkers.org

- **What Psalms can I use to kill a jinx?**

I mistakenly anointed myself with Crossing Oil and decided to give myself a Jinx Killer bath. What Psalms would be appropriate?
— GirlOnFire

Psalms 51 or Psalms 23 are both good for this. So is Peter 2:24: "He himself bore our sins in his body on the tree, that we might die to sin and live to righteousness. By his wounds you have been healed"
Also Deuteronomy 31:8:
"It is the Lord who goes before you. He will be with you; he will not leave you or forsake you. Do not fear or be dismayed."
Jinx Killer is one of my favourites for getting rid of accumulations of small irritations, thrown messes, as well as negative self-talk, but you do need to have that intent when doing the bath.
— Aura (M)

- **Is there any danger in using the Song of Solomon in love work?**

Are there any specific verses in The Song of Solomon I should avoid reading that may not be suitable for a love spell?
— cherish

No, you may read the entire Song of Solomon if you wish. However, there are probably certain passages that fit your situation more than others.
This book of the Bible reads like a poem with three different "voices": the man, the woman, and the chorus. The New International Version calls these Lover (man), Beloved (woman), and Friends. The Common English Bible uses Man, Woman, and Daughters of Jerusalem.
— Mama Micki (M)

The Song of Songs is often recommended for use in love spells. Note that it contains its own fabulous bath-herb blend at 4:14-15: "Spikenard and Saffron; Calamus and Cinnamon, with all trees of Frankincense; Myrrh and Aloes[wood], with all the chief spices: A fountain of gardens, a well of living waters, and streams from Lebanon."
— catherine yronwode (M, AIRR)

- **What Psalms can I use for a speedy financial windfall?**

What Psalms and petitions could I use to get a large sum of money quickly? I have Van Van Oil and other money drawing oils.
— Willa

I would work with Psalms 8 and 17. They have been good for me when I needed the money to pay for something like a bill. And Psalms 10, 21, 23, and 26 have always been good to me as well. I would also include Fast Luck Oil along with the other oils you mentioned.
— Starsinthesky7

Although fast money is great (particularly when unexpected bills or problems occur), preparing for the long haul by working with Wealthy Way, Money Stay With Me, and Steady Work spiritual supplies alongside regular readings of Psalms 23, 65, and 95 may be avenues to look at. And Wealthy Way products smell so absolutely divine it's hard to not want to fix pretty much everything in the house with them.
— Aura (M)

- **What scripture shall I use to cut and clear a man from the past?**

I'm still hurt and upset by a man from my past, a long time ago. I don't want to be missing him every once in a while, or having it interfere with my new relationship. I was thinking of purchasing a Cut and Clear Vigil Light. Would a petition saying something like, "Break [my name's] ties to past relationships and past lovers so she can move forward romantically with [new lover's name]" be appropriate?
— Sunshinegoddess

Your petition should be written in the first person. Say "my ties," not "her ties" and "so I can move forward," not "so she can move forward." You might also pray Isaiah 43:18-19:

"Remember ye not the former things, neither consider the things of old. Behold, I will do a new thing; now it shall spring forth; shall ye not know it? I will even make a way in the wilderness, and rivers in the desert."
— Mama Micki (M)

- **How do I choose prayers for my oils and herbs?**

I have noticed people talking about prayers that go with oils and herbs. Can someone tell me where I can find these prayers please?
— colliz

Look in your heart. There are no set prayers for the oils, but there are traditional prayers for certain intentions. Pray your intent as you employ the oils and you are on the right track. For inspiration, look to the Psalms.
— ConjureMan Ali (M, AIRR)

It is so important to speak from the heart; it's a place where the physical and spirit meet. It is from there that you pray the intent into the oil by speaking to it. Let your breath bring the oil to life. For me, after I do that then I will follow it up with a certain Psalm or a specific prayer such as the Our Father, for example. Though no matter what, speak from the heart.
— Papa Newt (M)

- **Which Psalm is better for Follow Me Girl work?**

I was able to order some Lucky Mojo Follow Me Girl Oil and I decided to read up on it. Lucky Mojo's page for Follow Me Girl suggests using the 23rd Psalm. However, if I were going to use Follow Me Girl for a reconciliation case, would it be better if I used Psalms 32? Or should I stick with the tradition and go with Psalms 23 still?
— AnnieB

Follow Me Girl spiritual supplies are often used in spells of attraction, in which case Psalms 23 is indicated, but you want to do a work of reconciliation, and in that case Psalms 32 would be exactly right for your situation, for it reads, *"Blessed is he whose transgression is forgiven, whose sin is covered."* I like that you are thinking of juxtaposing these Psalms, but I will say that when an oil is cited for use in a traditional way of working, it has a track record of proven results. You may want to use Follow Me Girl Oil and see where it gets you, but if you find that there is no movement, try Psalms 32 with the more appropriate Reconciliation Oil instead.
— Joseph Magnuson (M)

- **Do I have to read the whole Psalm suggested while bathing?**

When working with Psalms while taking a spiritual bath, is it acceptable to break up the Psalms into the verses that pertain to the issue or should I always read them from beginning to end?
— phelogeny

You can choose to work with just sections or with the whole Psalm. Try both out and see which feels right for the specific work you're doing.
— Aura (M)

Both methods of working with the Psalms are perfectly legitimate. Some pray the entirety of the Psalm while others only recite the verses pertaining to their situation, often over and over again like a mantra.

An alternative is to inscribe the pertinent verse on a candle or petition paper while reciting the entire Psalm out loud. This was a technique I picked up from a root doctor in Chicago who also was quite the kabbalist.
— ConjureMan Ali (M, AIRR)

- **How many times shall I repeat a prayer or Psalm?**

I was wondering how many times a prayer or Psalm was to be repeated during a spell. Is there a specific number or do I just say it once? I am a little confused by this, as I have heard several different recommendations.
— LoveisLove

It will both depend on the spell and the way you were taught. There can be variation from one job of work to another, as well as from one worker to another. Take the Fiery Wall of Protection Spell Kit, for instance. It provides materials for a traditional, elaborate, protective spell which ends with you saying Psalms 37 thirty-seven times as you cleanse your house. However, most spells call for a much smaller number of repetitions than thirty-seven, or for just one recital of a Psalm. Some spells specify just a short verse or two from a longer portion of Scripture and some simply call for you to carry out the actions of the spell while "praying for what you desire," and do not indicate any specific Biblical text at all.
— Miss Michaele (M, AIRR)

- **How do I keep a Psalm from getting wet during a spiritual bath?**

I don't have any of the Psalms memorized and I generally keep a print of the Psalm I am using near the bath tub and read it in between every head dousing. The momentum of the bathing would be better if I had it memorized, but that ain't gonna happen. So I always end up struggling trying to read from a wet piece of a paper.
— GirlOnFire

Get some plastic paper protectors at any store that sells office supplies.
— Mama Micki (M)

One word: Laminate.
— catherine yronwode (M, AIRR)

One more wrinkle: Get a cheap suction-cup hook. Stick it to your bathroom wall or shower door so that you can hang your laminated Psalm within easy view.
— Miss Michaele (M, AIRR)

- **Which Psalms are best to Cast Off Evil?**

I bought a white figural Adam Candle and Cast Off Evil Oil, to cast off ant problems my boyfriend has, whether it might be negativity, depression, or addiction. What would be an appropriate Psalm to use with my spell?
— Conjuremoon

Psalms 15 is great for that! It speaks of *"he that walketh uprightly, and worketh righteousness, and speaketh the truth in his heart"* and promises that *"he that doeth these things shall never be moved."* This Psalm not only helps to cast off evil but to protect against evil.
— ConjureMan Ali (M, AIRR)

James 4:7 (*"Submit yourselves therefore to God. Resist the devil, and he will flee from you"*) is not a Psalm, but it is a very powerful portion of Scripture and may be recited to drive away evil.
— Deacon Millett (M, AIRR)

- **Which Psalms for a Clarity and Psychic Vision bath?**

Which Psalm is best to use with a Clarity and Psychic Vision bath?
— virgosleo

I believe Psalms 89 is good. Recite verses 19-21, and substitute your own name for the name of David:
"Then thou spakest in vision to thy holy one, and saidst, I have laid help upon one that is mighty; I have exalted one chosen out of the people. I have found David my servant; with my holy oil have I anointed him: With whom my hand shall be established: mine arm also shall strengthen him."
— Miss Tammie Lee (M)

A passage found in both Joel 2:28-29 and Acts 2:17-18 is relevant:
"And it shall come to pass afterward, that I will pour out my spirit upon all flesh; and your sons and your daughter shall prophesy, your old men shall dream dreams, your young men shall see visions: and also upon the servants and upon the handmaids in those days will I pour out my spirit."
For Clarity, you can also cite Psalms 119:105:
"Thy word is a lamp unto my feet, and a light unto my path."
— Mama Micki (M)

- **How do you make an oil lamp?**

As someone who is new to this work, I'm not sure what people are talking about when they say they are making a lamp. What is this?
— CowboyInTheBoatofRa

As the Bible says in Psalms 119:105: *"Your word is a lamp to my feet and a light to my path."* For this and other reasons, oil lamps have a history of use in works of religious magic, prayer, petition, and spell casting, especially within the traditions of the African Diaspora, ceremonial magick, and Jewish mysticism. In hoodoo and conjure practice, a lamp such as this is a regular glass-reservoir kerosene lamp which has been fixed by adding minerals, herbs, roots, zoological curios, powders, and oils into the lamp's reservoir and then covering them with lamp fuel.
— ProfessorPorterfield

- **Why do uses of the Psalms differ from one worker to another?**

    Psalms 37 is one of the hoodoo standards for stopping gossip; it is an anti-evil-doers remedy. But in the book "Secrets of the Psalms" by Godfrey Selig, it is noted as a remedy for someone that drinks too much. This stood out because I use this Psalm quite a bit. What is the reason for this, if any, and what led to this happening?

    — BewitchingBelle

African-American folk magic practitioners have incorporated portions of Jewish kabbalistic folk magic within hoodoo, of which the book *Secrets of the Psalms* is a prime example. But hoodoo practitioners have also developed their own ways of working with the Psalms, which have been transmitted through family lineages and during conversations in candle shops — and some of these methods differ from classical Jewish usage of the Psalms. The variant prescriptions you noted for Psalms 37 are a good case in point.

Perhaps an analogy might help: The trumpet is a European brass instrument, developed for use in marching bands and large orchestras. African-American ways of using the trumpet in the performance of jazz are in many ways different from the classical European techniques. However, it is still correct to say that African-American jazz trumpeters obtained the instrument from European and European-American sources. And so it is with the Jewish Psalms; receiving the material, in English translation from originally Hebrew sources, African-American practitioners adapted the work to their own styles and requirements.

— catherine yronwode (M, AIRR)

- **How can I get a police record removed or pardoned?**

    What Psalm will aid me in obtaining a pardon for a false felony charge?
    — cougar

Pray Psalms 35 and Psalms 37 while you light brown candles that you've dressed with Court Case Oil on a honey jar for the governor of your state. Nine Sumac berries can be added to the honey for mercy of the court.

— ConjureMan Ali (M, AIRR)

- **Which Psalms are best for prosperity and getting work?**

As I've been doing things like dressing money, dressing business cards and letters, and doing spells for prosperity, I've found that I've wanted to add things to my work to concentrate my efforts more. I was wondering if anyone had suggestions on Psalms or prayers that I could add along with my specific requests. I've been using the 23rd Psalm, but I was wondering if there are other Psalms that are applicable to prosperity, getting work, keeping customers, and having money stay with me. Thanks.
— Jude423

Psalms 8 (*"O Lord, our Lord, how excellent is thy name in all the earth!"*) is good for success in business, while Psalms 75 (*"Unto thee, O God, do we give thanks"*) can be used to encourage hiring.
— thelightfantastic

For money I read Psalms 119: 17-24. I hope this helps…
— True Believer

I read Deuteronomy 28 for my money spells. It talks about God's blessings over His people, always prospering, being the head and not the tail, and things to that nature: *"And the Lord shall make thee plenteous in goods, in the fruit of thy body, and in the fruit of thy cattle, and in the fruit of thy ground."* Look it up and see if you feel connected to it.
— interested

- **Which Scripture is said for the return of money owed?**

How do I get back money that was taken from me?
— debra1961

I suggest that you work with a white candle, dressed with Pay Me Oil and inscribed with Proverbs 3:28: *"Say not unto thy neighbour, 'Go, and come again, and to morrow I will give;' when thou hast it by thee."* While this candle is burning go and telephone or text the person and ask for your money. If you can't connect that way, write a letter on paper and mail it.
— catherine yronwode

- **Must I use the King James Bible?**

Is it important to use the King James Version of the Bible when praying the Psalms?

— barat

The choice of a Bible is about culture and family traditions — the family traditions and culture of real, living people. If you are not a member of African-American culture, but want to become a part of it, or work within its traditions, meet with the culture as best you can, join a church, and read the Bible you are given.

I learned on the King James Version in the black churches I attended and from the preachers and conjure workers and spiritual ladies who taught me, so I stick with that translation of the Bible.

Until the Jewish Study Bible was published, most Jews used the King James Bible when reading the Tanakh in English. I was taught by my Jewish family and by many other Jews that the King James Version was a very accurate translation of the Hebrew Tanakh. The English Haggadahs for Pesach we had used the King James Version, as did our side-by-side (Hebrew/English) rendition of the Tehillim (Psalms).

Here's a modern Jewish scholar's take on the subject of accuracy. It comes from an essay titled "Jewish Translations of the Bible" by Leonard J. Greenspoon, published in *The Jewish Study Bible* (Jewish Publication Society / Oxford University Press, 2004)./

"The cadence, vocabulary, and overall structure of KJV strongly resemble the Hebrew original. Any number of memorable turns of phrases ('tender mercies,' Psalms 25:6 and elsewhere) or lingering verbal pictures ('the face of the waters,' Genesis 1:2, and 'the Lord make his face to shine upon thee,' Numbers 6:26) we associate with KJV are in fact quite literal renderings of the Hebrew lost in freer translations into English or other modern languages."

— catherine yronwode (M, AIRR)

KJV is the best translation, just over all. It is the most lyrical and poetic of the lot. The newer translations are good for some things but if you're looking for poetry and tradition, the KJV is the one to go with.

— cognitivedissonance

- **How can we protect against evil spirits in dreams?**

Can spirits visit us in dreams, and can a person open the doorway of negativity to let spirits or negativity enter a home? If so, how can we protect ourselves against this?
— Freja

Yes, it's entirely possible to send dreams to people, for good or for ill. You can protect yourself against negative dreams by keeping a Bible open to a protection Psalm under your pillow or under your bed, with a pair of open scissors or a sharp knife laid on it. Psalms 91, 121, and 126 most often cited, but Colossians 1:20 (*"I rebuke all spirits of torment and fear because I have peace through the blood of Jesus"*) is also beneficial.
— Miss Michaele (M, AIRR)

- **How do I make payment to Jesus?**

If Jesus helps you with an issue, what is the payment you give, analogous to giving pound cake for Saint Expedite or publicly thanking Saint Jude? Maybe red wine? Donating to a Catholic church?
— heartexalted

Jesus is not a "saint." According to Christian belief he is the Son of God (or God the Son). He does not require payment.

However, consider this passage from Matthew 25:34-40:

"Then shall the King say unto them on his right hand, Come, ye blessed of my Father, inherit the kingdom prepared for you from the foundation of the world: For I was an hungred, and ye gave me meat: I was thirsty, and ye gave me drink: I was a stranger, and ye took me in: Naked, and ye clothed me: I was sick, and ye visited me: I was in prison, and ye came unto me. Then shall the righteous answer him, saying, Lord, when saw we thee an hungred, and fed thee? or thirsty, and gave thee drink? When saw we thee a stranger, and took thee in? or naked, and clothed thee? Or when saw we thee sick, or in prison, and came unto thee? And the King shall answer and say unto them, Verily I say unto you, Inasmuch as ye have done it unto one of the least of these my brethren, ye have done it unto me."
— Mama Micki (M)

- **Any Psalms or prayers to attract gay men?**

Are there any Psalms that would help me with attracting gay men? I have Kiss Me Now, Look Me Over, and Follow Me Boy Oil as well.
— Soluna

Start with an Attraction, Look Me Over, or Dixie Love Vigil Candle with some dried lavender in or around it.

Many have success with Psalms 138 *("I will praise thee with my whole heart")*. I would also recite Ecclesiastes 4:9-12:

"Two are better than one; because they have a good reward for their labour. For if they fall, the one will lift up his fellow: but woe to him that is alone when he falleth; for he hath not another to help him up. Again, if two lie together, then they have heat: but how can one be warm alone?"

You could also add the following, from the Song of Solomon 5:2-8

"I sleep, but my heart waketh: it is the voice of my beloved that knocketh, saying, Open to me, my sister, my love, my dove, my undefiled: for my head is filled with dew, and my locks with the drops of the night

I have put off my coat; how shall I put it on? I have washed my feet; how shall I defile them?

My beloved put in his hand by the hole of the door, and my bowels were moved for him.

I rose up to open to my beloved; and my hands dropped with Myrrh, and my fingers with sweet smelling Myrrh, upon the handles of the lock.
— HecatesHeart

Although one can find Bible texts that seem condemnatory of gay love, I have always taken comfort in the frank and openly loving relationship between Jonathan, the son of the evil King Saul, and David, the shepherd boy who one day would be king. In 1 Samuel 18:1 we read, *"And it came to pass, when he had made an end of speaking unto Saul, that the soul of Jonathan was knit with the soul of David, and Jonathan loved him as his own soul."* Later, the apparently bisexual David says this of his gay lover Jonathan in 2 Samuel 1:26, *"I am distressed for thee, my brother Jonathan: very pleasant hast thou been unto me: thy love to me was wonderful, passing the love of women."*
— nagasiva yronwode (M)

- **Books on hoodoo and religion?**

I would love any book recommendations that y'all might have, especially on the religious aspects of hoodoo.

— Magnolia

I would recommend the following books on religion and rootwork:
Key of Solomon the King attributed to Solomon
The 6th and 7th Books of Moses attributed to Moses
Secrets of the Psalms by Godfrey A. Selig
Pow-Wows, or The Long-Lost Friend by John George Hohman
18 Lost Years of Jesus by Lloyd Kenyon Jones
Ten Lost Books of the Prophets by Lewis de Claremont
The Magic Formula for Successful Prayer by Mikhail Strabo
How to Conduct a Candle Light Service by Mikhail Strabo
The Master Book of Candle Burning by Henri Gamache
Protection Against Evil by Henri Gamache
The Long-Lost 8th, 9th, and 10th Books of Moses by Henri Gamache
Powers of the Psalms by Anna Riva
Helping Yourself with Selected Prayers by Anna Riva
375 Ways To Use Psalms by Anna Riva

The first four titles span more than 700 years, but the rest are 20th century conjure classics. All of them are available in hoodoo candle shops.

— Leah Rivera (M, AIRR)

- **How to Remove a Generational Curse on a Family?**

Is it possible for hexes to affect a family or multiple generations? Can they affect pregnant women or unborn children? If so, what steps should I take?

— Windprancer

Yes, generational curses do exist. To break their hold over a family, I was taught to recite 1 Chronicles 1:1-28 from Adam through the sons of Abraham, followed by a recitation of the family's names, going seven generations back, if possible, followed by the entirety of Psalms 25. You can pray this while working with an Uncrossing Spell Kit.

— ConjureMan Ali (M, AIRR)

- **Is High Altar Oil traditional to the Bible?**

I've been wondering, if High Altar Oil, a traditional hoodoo oil, comes from the Bible? Also, is 7-11 Holy Oil a substitute for High Altar Oil?
— Apo

High Altar Oil, also spelled Hi-Altar Oil — and also known in traditional hoodoo shops as 7-11 Holy Oil, Holy Oil, Bible Oil, Exodus Oil, Temple Oil, and Abramelin Oil — all derive from the formula given in the Bible, in the Book of Exodus. Because that oil was specified to be made and used only on the Temple altar of the Jews, and the Temple was destroyed, it is the custom of Jewish pharmacists and apothecaries to make slightly "off-spec" versions, incorporating minor, almost indistinguishable, differences from the original recipe and to give the resultant oil names that imply, but do not directly state, that this is the true Holy Oil of the Temple.

For my own manufactory, i have settled on a famous name for this compound: 7-11 Holy Oil. This name came out of a Chicago pharmacy formulary of the 1930s, and — like all the others listed above — it is essentially a close but not exact copy of the Biblical Holy Oil.
— catherine yronwode (M, AIRR)

- **How to do a Road Opening with the Bible?**

I heard that the Bible is the great Road Opener and clearer, but how?
— coastwitch

In doing work such as this, you may first wish to cut ties to the hindrances of the past, and then to open your paths to new opportunities..

Use Cut and Clear supplies to make a clean break with past events or people, reciting over your work Isaiah 43:18-19: *"Remember ye not the former things, neither consider the things of old. Behold, I will do a new thing; now it shall spring forth; shall ye not know it? I will even make a way in the wilderness, and rivers in the desert"*

Then use Road Opener supplies to bring about forward motion, reciting Isaiah 45:2: *"I will go before thee, and make the crooked places straight: I will break in pieces the gates of brass, and cut in sunder the bars of iron"*
— Mama Micki (M)

ONE LAST CURIOSITY: THE SOLDIER'S BIBLE

During the 1930s, Rev. Harry Hyatt collected the saying that a deck of cards represents every book in the Bible from Genesis to Revelation. His informant was describing a very old recitation, which in America had been told about the Civil War, the Spanish-American War, and the First World War — and would later be told about the Second World War, the Korean War, the Vietnam War, and the wars in Iraq and Afghanistan. In fact the story has been told about European wars back to the 18th century — for it is found in the 1762 household ledger of Mary Bacon, an English farmwife.

This version was recorded by T. Texas Tyler in 1948 as "Deck of Cards":

Friends, this is T. Texas Tyler, with a strange story about a soldier boy and a deck of cards.

During the North African campaign, a bunch of soldier boys had been on a long hike and they arrived in a little town called Casino. The next morning being Sunday, several of the boys went to church. A Sergeant commanded the boys in church and after the Chaplain had read the prayer, the text was taken up next. Those of the boys who had a prayer book took them out, but this one boy had only a deck of cards, and so he spread them out.

The Sergeant saw the cards and said, "Soldier, put away those cards."

After the services was over, the soldier was taken prisoner and brought before the Provost Marshall.

The Marshall said, "Sergeant, why have you brought this man here?"

"For playing cards in church, Sir."

"And what have you to say for yourself, son?"

"Much, Sir," replied the soldier.

The Marshall said, "I hope so, for if not, I shall punish you more than any man was ever punished."

The soldier said, "Sir, I have been on the march for about six days. I have neither a Bible nor a prayer book, but I hope to satisfy you, Sir, with the purity of my intentions."

With that, the boy started his story:

"You see, Sir, when I look at the Ace, it reminds me that there is but one God.

And the Deuce reminds me that the Bible is divided into two parts, the Old and the New Testaments.

And when I see the Trey, I think of the Father, the Son, and the Holy Ghost.

And when I see the Four, I think of the four Evangelists who preached the Gospel; there was Matthew, Mark, Luke, and John.

And when I see the Five, it reminds me of the five wise virgins who trimmed their lamps; there were ten of them: five were wise and were saved, five were foolish and were shut out.

And when I see the Six, it reminds me that in six days, God made this great heaven and earth.

When I see the Seven, it reminds me that on the seventh day, God rested from His great work.

And when I see the Eight, I think of the eight righteous persons God saved when He destroyed this earth; there was Noah, his wife, their three sons, and their wives.

And when I see the Nine, I think of the lepers our Saviour cleansed, and nine out of the ten didn't even thank Him.

When I see the Ten, I think of the Ten Commandments God handed down to Moses on a table of stone.

When I see the King, it reminds me there is but one King of Heaven, God Almighty.

And when I see the Queen, I think of the Blessed Virgin Mary, who is Queen of Heaven.

And the Jack or Knave is the Devil.

When I count the number of spots on a deck of cards, I find 365, the number of days in a year.

There's 52 cards, the number of weeks in a year.

There's 4 suits, the number of weeks in a month.

There's 12 picture cards, the number of months in a year.

There's 13 tricks, the number of weeks in a quarter.

So you see, Sir, my pack of cards serves me as a Bible, Almanac, and Prayer Book."

And friends, this story is true. I know — because I was … that soldier.

And with this we leave you, girded by the Sacred Secrets of Scriptural Sorcery. For now YOU are "that soldier," armed and ready to face all that would come against you and attempt to thwart you. So go out, friends, and attain the summit of the mountain, that you too might look out and see your own Promised Land.

— Miss Michaele and Prof. C. D. Porterfield

Bibliography

The Holy Bible: King James Version, Revised Edition. Thomas Nelson, Inc. 1976.
ANDERSON, Jeffrey E. *Conjure in African American Society.* Louisiana State University Press, 2001.
[ALBERTS MAGNUS; attributed]. *Albertus Magnus, Being the Approved, Verified, Sympathetic and Natural Egyptian Secrets or White and Black Art for Man and Beast, Revealing the Forbidden Knowledge and Mysteries of Ancient Philosophers.* [1478 in German; the first English edition appeared in 1725.]
    BERRY, Jason. *The Spirit of Black Hawk: A Mystery of Africans and Indians.* University Press of Mississippi, 1995.
    CHIREAU, Yvonne P. *Black Magic: Religion and the African American Conjuring Tradition.* University of California Press, 2006.
    DE CLAREMONT, Lewis. *Legends of Incense, Herb, and Oil Magic.* Oracle Publishing Co., 1936.
    GAMACHE, Henri. *Mystery of the Long Lost 8th, 9th and 10th Books of Moses Together With the Legend That Was of Moses and 44 Secret Keys to Universal Power.* Sheldon, 1948.
    ----------. *The Master Book of Candle Burning.* Dorene Publishing, 1942.
    ----------. *The Master Key to Occult Secrets.* Open Door Publishing Company, 1945.
    HASKINS, Jim. *Voodoo and Hoodoo: the Craft as Revealed by Traditional Practitioners.* Scarborough House, 1978.
    HOHMAN, [Johann Georg]. *Pow-Wows or The Long Lost Friend.* Stein, 1935. [Reprints *The Long Secreted Friend or A True and Christian Information for Everybody; Containing Wonderful and Approved Remedies and Arts for Men and Beasts.* John George Hohman, 1846]
    HURSTON, Zora Neale. *Hoodoo in America.* Journal of American Folklore, Vol. 44, 1931.
    ----------. *Mules and Men.* J.B. Lippincott, 1935. Reprinted, Harper Collins, 1990.
    HYATT, Harry Middleton. *Hoodoo - Conjuration - Witchcraft - Rootwork.* [Five Vols.] Memoirs of the Alma Egan Hyatt Foundation, 1970-78.
    ----------. *Folklore of Adams County, Illinois.* Memoirs of the Alma Egan Hyatt Foundation, 1935.
    JACOBS, Claude F., and Andrew J. Kaslow. *The Spiritual Churches of New Orleans: Origins, Beliefs, And Rituals Of An African-American Religion.* University of Tennessee Press, 2001.
    JOHNSON, F. Roy. *The Fabled Doctor Jim Jordan, a Story of Conjure.* Johnson Publishing Co, 1963.
    LAFOREST, Aura. *Hoodoo Spiritual Baths: Cleansing Conjure with Washes and Waters.* Lucky Mojo Curio Co., 2014.
    LONG, Carolyn Morrow. *Spiritual Merchants: Religion, Magic, and Commerce.* University of Tennessee Press, 2001.
    MATHERS, Samuel Liddell MacGregor. *The Key of Solomon the King (Clavicula Salomonis).* George Redway, 1888.
    [MOSES; attributed] *The Sixth and Seventh Books of Moses.* Wehman Brothers, 1880. [translated from the German edition of 1865 published by Johann Scheible.]
    PETERSON, Joseph H. *The Lesser Key of Solomon.* Weiser, 2001.
    PUCKETT, Newbell Niles. *Folk Beliefs of the Southern Negro.* University of North Carolina Press, 1926.
    RABO, Rajah [Carl Z. Talbot]. *Pick 'Em Dream Book.* Oak Sales, 1953.
    SELIG, Godfrey. *Secrets of the Psalms: A Fragment of the Practical Kabbalah.* [n.p.], [c. 1788].
    SONNY BOY [pseudonym]. *King Solomon's Alleged Guide to Success? Power!* Sonny Boy Products, [c.1960].
    STRABO, Mikhail [Sydney J. R. Steiner]. *The Magic Formula for Successful Prayer.* Guidance House, 1942.
    PETERSON, Joseph. *The Sixth and Seventh Books of Moses.* Ibis Press, 2008.
    TRACHTENBERG, Joshua. *Jewish Magic and Superstition: A Study in Folk Religion.* Behrman's Jewish Book House, 1939.
    YRONWODE, Catherine. *Hoodoo Herb and Root Magic: A Materia Magica of African-American Conjure.* Lucky Mojo Curio Co., 2002.
    ---------- and Mikhail Strabo [Sydney J. R. Steiner]. *The Art of Hoodoo Candle Magic.* Missionary Independent Spiritual Church, 2013.